I0458410

"Dina Shapiro has made change management easy with her Change Management for Marketers *program—even for those of us who aren't in marketing! The antithesis of a dense college marketing textbook, her book is a fast read and a very digestible road map of how companies and employees may successfully implement internal transformations.*"

—Michelle Richmond
News and Documentary Producer

"Change Management for Marketers *simplifies things and helps readers see that transformation is impossible. That if done with intention and with focus on the humans involved, the outcomes will be as planned! This book shows that businesses are run by humans, and encourages involving them and making them feel valued and a part of the process because they are legitimately part of the solution!!*"

—Jay Pila, CSL
Outsourced VP of Sales

"The need for a thoughtful marketing transformation is often overlooked, simply because marketers are used to being in service of their company, versus turning the focus on themselves. But the ones who commit to the journey are rewarded with greater effectiveness, efficiency, and creativity. This book provides a clear, straightforward process, and actionable tools and examples so marketers never have to start with a blank page. Shapiro's perspective is invaluable given that she has been on all sides of the equation: head of marketing at large companies, a change management consultant, a professor of marketing, and a managing director at an agency. She brings all this experience to the book while making a bear of an undertaking feel fun and manageable."

—Nicole Ferry
Partner, Chief Strategy Officer, Sullivan

"Dina's Shapiro's debut book hits the mark with its persuasive use of storytelling, authentic voice and compelling insights around how to manage change in a corporate environment. Her strategy of 'placing people at the heart of change' illustrates Dina's emotional intelligence and how she is guided by empathy in her professional interactions. Change Management for Marketers or CMfM, is an uplifting and sensible book that reminds us that marketers can, indeed, be the 'masters of change.'"

—Felicia A. Foster
Marketing Consultant and Advertising Account Director

CHANGE MANAGEMENT
FOR
MARKETERS

CHANGE MANAGEMENT FOR MARKETERS

Internal Transformations Made Easy

DINA L. SHAPIRO

THIN LEAF PRESS | LOS ANGELES

Library of Congress Cataloging-in-Publication Data
Name: Shapiro, Dina L., Author
Title: *Change Management for Marketers: Internal Transformations Made Easy.*
LCCN: 2024926181

ISBN 978-1-953183-68-2 (hardcover) | 978-1-953183-67-5 (paperback)
ISBN 978-1-953183-66-8 (eBook) | 978-1-953183-69-9 (audiobook)

Change Management, Business, Professional Development
Cover Design: 100 Covers, Azist
Interior Illustrations: Azist
Interior Design: Rochelle Mensidor
Editors: Erik Seversen, Dhanliza Cellona
Thin Leaf Press
Los Angeles

THIN
LEAF

For Stephen Irwin Shapiro

August 27, 1937 — May 29, 2023

I know you're proud, Dad.

CONTENTS

INTRODUCTION

Why I Wrote This Book and How It Will Help You

Okay, I'll say it. Marketing transformations suck. Nobody wants to do them.

In business, the word "transformation" implies that something isn't working, so you better do something big to fix it, like right now. I don't know anyone who wakes up in the morning saying, "I can't wait to do a marketing transformation!"

In fact, there's a lot of **marketing transformation fatigue** going on. I've conducted many interviews on this topic. After the eye roll, here's what people say when I ask them to describe marketing transformations:

- *"Anxiety"*
- *"Unclear"*
- *"Daunting"*
- *"Resistance"*
- *"Traumatic"*
- *"Exhausting"*
- *"Constant frustration"*
- *"Excruciatingly difficult"*
- *"The spirit is willing, but the flesh is weak."*

- *"Everyone is annoyed and passive-aggressive."*
- *"Feel like we get lost in this tunnel and can't get out."*
- *"People feel excited and enthusiastic at first, but it wears off over time."*

Any of this sound familiar to you? I am here to tell you that it does **not** have to be that painful. **There is a better way.**

Hi, I'm Dina Shapiro. I want to help you navigate the process of **change management for marketing transformations.** I will help you through it with less pain, in less time, with better outcomes, and some lightheartedness.

I wrote this book for **client-side marketers who need change management for marketing transformations.** This book is equally helpful for **partners** of client-side marketers including internal and external agencies, internal change managers, and external change management consultants.

I think of change management like a big pizza pie. There are lots of slices, most of which are for organization-wide initiatives that affect all employees, like when HR creates a new performance appraisal process, or IT switches software vendors for shared documents. **In this book**, we will focus on **only one** of the many slices of the change management pizza pie: **change management for marketing transformations.**

After reading this book, you will be able to:

- **Define** change management specific to marketing transformations and how it **differs** from organization-wide change management.
- Recognize how **your amazing marketing skills, experience, and traits** enable you to **lead** change management for marketing transformations.

- **Empathize** with your colleagues' fear of change and help them **overcome** their barriers.
- Create an insightful **Employee Change Journey Map** including personas, stages, messaging, and touch points.
- Write an inspiring **Change Management Brief** for everyone involved in the creation and approval of change story communications and resources, such as creative directors, writers, graphic designers, change leaders, and decision-makers.
- Create a marketing transformation change management **process** including key **steps, collaboration** with internal and external stakeholders, and **measurement and optimization** of change management strategies and tactics.
- Tackle **the first 90 days** of your change management plan implementation.

Dr. Martin Luther King, Jr. said, *"Change does not roll in on the wheels of inevitability but comes through continuous struggle."*

Despite humans being programmed for change (more about this in chapter 2), people often resist, fear, or feel threatened by change. Dr. King's quote is a powerful reminder that change is hard, and it does not happen on its own. Navigating change requires time and effort.

Are you ready for some insight and inspiration? Let's keep going.

MARKETING TRANSFORMATIONS
Definition and Examples

Before we dive into the first chapter, let's define "marketing transformations" and review how marketing transformation examples are used in this book.

I'll paraphrase the definition of "transformation" from Cambridge Dictionary and Merriam-Webster Dictionary and place it into the context of marketing:

A marketing transformation is a gradual series of actions to reinvent and improve marketing capabilities, technologies, strategies, processes, organization, or culture.

Let's break down that definition:

Gradual series of actions: A marketing transformation does not happen overnight. It takes **time** and often launches in phases or requires ongoing upgrades or optimizations.

Reinvent and improve: A marketing transformation is not a small, little change. It's a big, **dramatic** change with a **purpose**.

Marketing capabilities, technologies, strategies, processes, organization, or culture represent common types of marketing transformations, which as you can see, include quite a range! Examples include strategic shifts such as new processes or a brand repositioning, digital and technology improvements such as new customer data management software, leadership changes, or company mergers and acquisitions.

Each chapter in this book includes a **case study** about **internal change management** for a marketing transformation to **demonstrate** key learning points. These case studies include a **representative range** of marketing transformation types, which is not intended to be a complete list.

This book does not assess or judge any of the mentioned marketing transformations. Rather, we focus on **change management for** the transformation, meaning, we pick up *after* the decision to proceed with the transformation.

All change management ideas, frameworks, processes, and templates shared in this book will improve the success of **any type** of marketing transformation.

*"Successful change management requires **traction.**"*

—Dina Shapiro

CHAPTER 1

CHANGE MANAGEMENT

What Is It and Why Does It Matter?

"Be the change you wish to see in the world."
—Mahatma Ghandi

 LEARNING OBJECTIVES

After reading this chapter, you will be able to define change management for marketing transformations and recognize its importance for marketing transformations to succeed.

 DEFINITION OF CHANGE MANAGEMENT FOR MARKETING TRANSFORMATIONS

There are billions (yes, billions) of search results for the definition of change management. I'm exhausted even thinking about them!

I won't take on every one of those billions of definitions for the entire change management pizza pie.

Our definition in this book focuses on our *one slice* of the change management pizza pie:

Change management is a process to advocate for the human side of a marketing transformation.

Let's break down that definition:

Process: People have told me that they feel like, *"I already have so many processes. Stop. Please. I can't. You want me to take on yet one more process?!"* In short, yes. Change management requires a **series of gradual, deliberate, systematic actions** to move forward toward a positive outcome, which in our case, is adoption and sustainability of a marketing transformation.

Advocate: Successful change management gains **traction** through **support, participation,** and **recommendations.** Advocacy is most credible from a range of tenure, levels, disciplines, and personality types involved with the transformation. Advocacy from leadership is critical to success; however, it alone is not sufficient to create a change movement.

Human: We need to guide those impacted by the change with **empathy,** to envision what the transformation is like from **their** perspective. This insight helps us place **people at the heart of the change,** so we share relevant information and create an engaging experience throughout their change journey.

IMPORTANCE OF CHANGE MANAGEMENT FOR MARKETING TRANSFORMATIONS

Have you heard the saying, "*the only constant in life is change*"? All organizations (not just yours) experience changes. According to Gartner, a world-leading research and advisory company, 82% of marketing leaders report that their organization is **currently undergoing change management**, and nearly 75% of organizations expect to have **even more** change in the future.

Marketing transformations can be **proactive** or **reactive**. For example, a consumer-packaged goods company may *proactively* innovate its packaging to be more sustainable, or it could *reactively* upgrade its data storage technology due to a customer data privacy issue.

Almost all organizations are experiencing transformations. So all these organizations need **change management** for their **marketing transformation to succeed**.

 ## WHY MOST CHANGE INITIATIVES FAIL

According to many sources including Harvard Business Review, a publishing affiliate of Harvard Business School, and McKinsey, a global management consultancy, **only about 1/3 of transformations succeed**.

What?!

Seriously?!

Yes. About **70%** of organizational transformations **fail**.

Why? Because of change *mismanagement* for employees, such as:

- They're **not included** in the process; the change happens "to" them, not "with" them.
- They have no **training.**
- There is inadequate communication about the transformation **purpose** or **benefits.**
- Leaders are not in tune with what people need to **hear from them directly.**
- No **timeline** is shared for the transformation or when people are expected to modify their responsibilities or behaviors.
- There is no plan or assistance to **overcome** change obstacles.
- There is no **measurement** or optimization of the change management.

I know, I know, lots of mistakes being made out there! And this is just a partial list. Sigh.

 APPLICATION OF WHAT WE HAVE LEARNED: *Demonstrating the Importance of Change Management*

This is a case study about **the importance of change management** for a brand transformation.

The executive team of a health insurance company updated their company's vision and values.

The CMO, Chris, led the creation of the brand transformation to align with the new company direction. The brand was repositioned to support the new company vision, and be more competitive and relevant. The brand guidelines, specifically the brand tone and personality, were rewritten to reflect the new company values.

The work itself, meaning the new brand positioning and guidelines, was solid.

So what *was* the problem? **No change management for the brand transformation!**

In short, Chris made a few mistakes. Chris only included a few, select, favored people to work on the project. Other impacted stakeholders were **excluded**, such as marketers and creative teams who create campaigns, customer service representatives who field calls and chats with customers, and HR recruiters who engage prospective employees. Chris did **not** communicate the **benefits or rationale** for the new brand positioning and guidelines, or how they support the new company vision and values. Chris **provided no training,** so nobody understood what they needed to do differently moving forward.

As a result, the brand transformation *failed to gain traction*.

People were confused, upset, questioned what the changes meant for them, and did not advocate for the brand transformation.

Yeah, this situation went south. In fact, Chris was removed from their position after this incident.

You can easily **avoid these mistakes** so your transformations will succeed. I'll share ideas for *how to use change management* to drive success of marketing transformation in chapters 5 — 13. Stay with me.

 **INSIDER TIP**

You can be a really smart marketer but **fail to gain transformation adoption** due to **change *mismanagement*.** The simple act of *who* you bring into the process can make or break your success. (Yes, really.) When people *feel included* in the change, your transformation gains *traction*. **Change management** for marketing transformations requires including the right people, at the right time, in the right way. More about inclusiveness "why" and "how" are sprinkled throughout this book, with a heavy up in chapter 12.

 KEY TAKEAWAYS

Let's summarize key takeaways for change management and why it matters:

1. Our definition of change management is **a process to advocate for the human side of a marketing transformation.**
2. Most organizations experience changes and will continue to experience even **more changes** soon, creating the need for more and better change management.
3. **Most organization transformations fail** due to change *mismanagement*.

But don't despair! The rest of this book describes how you can successfully manage change, so **you won't** be in that 70% failure rate. Let's read on.

*"We are all **capable of change.**"*

—Dina Shapiro

CHAPTER 2

THE HUMAN CHEMISTRY OF CHANGE

How to Overcome Fear of Marketing Transformations

"Whenever you feel afraid, just remember. Courage is the root of change – and change is what we're chemically designed to do."
—Bonnie Garmus

 LEARNING OBJECTIVES

After reading this chapter, you will be able to describe the human chemistry of change, why we fear change, and how to overcome the fear of change.

THE HUMAN CHEMISTRY OF CHANGE

Human beings, every one of us, are *chemically programmed to change*. However, we often fear and avoid change. Why the disconnect?

Allow me to explain.

Let's start with the word "chemistry," which has both **science** and **relationship** definitions. I will paraphrase both definitions from Cambridge Dictionary and Merriam-Webster Dictionary.

The **science** definition of chemistry is how substances **react** with one another and **transform**. This is the type of chemistry you may have studied in school, such as "Chemistry 101."

The **relationship** definition of chemistry is a quality that exists when people are **empathetic, bond** with one another, and **engage** in a productive relationship. This is the type of chemistry you may hear about at work, such as a "high performing team that has good chemistry."

Hold on, there's more.

According to an interview conducted by NPR, an independent, nonprofit media organization, with Howard Markel, MD, PhD, physician, medical educator, and historian of medicine at The University of Michigan, the origin of the word chemistry is believed by most to be derived from the Greek word "khemeia" or "chemia," which means "pouring **together** or **infusion**." Fast forward about 2,000 years to the modern definition of the word chemistry, which is "how matter **changes** forms by means of chemical **reactions**."

Let's collate those **bolded** words from above
and look at them all together:

React • Transform • Empathy • Bond • Engage •
Together • Infusion • Change

Are you starting to see the connection between chemistry +
change + humans? Go back and read those words gain.

I'm going to add one more dimension to chemistry—**human
chemistry**—that we are all chemically and physically *born
to change* throughout our lives. We are born small and with
just the basic human abilities, such as to sleep, cry, eat,
smile, laugh, pee, and poop (sometimes more than one of
these at the same time; you know a baby). Then our bodies
grow, appearances change, brains develop, and abilities grow
and improve, and so on. We evolve from babies to children,
teenagers, adults, and then seniors. **Our bodies change
from the day we are born until the day we pass on.** (People
much smarter than me can explain the science of how our
bodies change chemically and physically. This is beyond my
purview, but I think you get my point that **we humans are
designed to change**.)

 ## WHY WE FEAR CHANGE

Let's go back to Bonnie's quote from the beginning of this
chapter: *"Whenever you feel **afraid**, just remember. Courage
is the root of **change**—and **change** is what we're chemically
designed to do."* Bonnie associates the word "afraid" with
change. She understands that people fear change, despite
people being born to change.

Why is this? Why do we fear change? Why, why, why?

There are tons of books, articles, social media posts, and blogs that have lengthy, complicated, psychobabble lists about the reasons people fear change and why employees fear transformations.

I'll sum up the reason why people fear change in one word: **UNCERTAINTY.**

Uncertainty is a common thread among people involved in marketing transformations.

Allow me to demonstrate. I'll insert the phrase, *"I feel uncertain"* in front of common phrases people have shared with me about their marketing transformation experiences:

- I feel *uncertain*...why this is happening.
- I feel *uncertain*...how this will affect my daily routine.
- I feel *uncertain*...if I will still be able to perform my job well.
- I feel *uncertain*...about my job security.
- I feel *uncertain*...because nobody asked me if I agree with or want this.
- I feel *uncertain*...about the transformation timing.
- I feel *uncertain*...what training will be provided.
- I feel *uncertain*...if I still fit in.
- I feel *uncertain*...about what's coming next.
- I feel *uncertain*...and alone.

Why do employees fear marketing transformations? **Uncertainty.**

When I was a marketing practitioner, I felt uncertain about marketing transformations. I identify with lots of things on the list we just reviewed above. Do you?

HOW TO OVERCOME UNCERTAINTY

Here's an interesting point I discovered in my research about **uncertainty.**

According to the National Institute of Health (NIH) National Library of Medicine (NLM), the world's largest biomedical library founded in 1836, neuroscience shows that we **struggle to tolerate uncertainty because our brain associates uncertainty with an error.**

When we feel uncertain about something—like a marketing transformation—our brain wants to *correct* that uncertainty that it registers as an error so we can feel comfortable again.

So basically, change management for marketing transformations needs to **mitigate people's feelings of uncertainty** so they can feel comfortable and progress positively toward adoption and sustainability.

APPLICATION OF WHAT WE HAVE LEARNED: *Mitigating Uncertainty About a Transformation*

This is a case study about Abigail, a website and mobile app designer who works at a hotel. She felt **uncertain** about an upcoming software transformation.

Abigail's marketing team was losing opportunities to convert prospects from their website and mobile app due to a poor user experience (UX). Her team recognized the problems and analyzed ways to resolve customer complaints through UX research and a competitive analysis. They tested a couple of rough UX improvements with a representative customer sample. They prepared a proposal for leadership including three options for how to improve the website and mobile app UX, vendors to consider with pros and cons of each, and proposed logistics. They were excited to schedule a meeting to present their recommendation.

The next thing they knew, they heard that the leadership team *already* decided which vendor to hire and software to implement and approved the budget and schedule.

The team was shocked! They felt excluded and rejected. They could not understand why they were not consulted given their expertise and everyday experience with the website and mobile app. They felt like the change was happening "to" them, not "with" them. A case of change *mismanagement*.

They felt **uncertain** about:

> ...how this transformation would launch and roll out.

> ...what specific UX changes would be implemented.

> ...if prospective customers would feel better about the website and mobile app changes.

> ...how the team's roles and responsibilities would change.

> ...if the team would suffer job eliminations.

> ...why they were excluded.

Because their brains registered all these uncertainties as **errors**, people felt *uncomfortable, fearful, demotivated, disrespected,* and *unimportant.* Whispers started about people interviewing at other companies.

Yikes.

Ouch.

Painful.

Alas, I cannot end this story on a bad note!

Let's **rewrite** Abigail's story to see *how effective change management could turn the tide.*

In a perfect world, leadership would have included Abigail's team, the subject matter experts, from the beginning and asked them to lead the process.

But I propose that we do not begin our re-written story there. Let's make this realistic and a little more challenging than a perfect world scenario since we live in an imperfect world.

Let's start our rewritten story when leadership behaved in a not-so-great way. They made decisions and dictated the change. They excluded people. They did not consult the subject matter experts. They did not recognize or account for the daily implications of the transformation.

What could Abigail do under these circumstances? She wants the transformation to launch successfully. She wants her team to stay at the company and adopt and sustain the changes. She wants her team and prospective customers to benefit from the changes.

Abigail had a productive and trusting relationship with David, one of the people on the leadership team. She requested a 1:1 meeting with him to understand the rationale for their decisions, benefits of the chosen software and vendor, and budget and schedule expectations. She did not debate. She was not defensive. She was open and listened actively. (After all, these decisions were already made, right?)

Abigail diplomatically shared with David all the uncertainties that she and her team were feeling. They brainstormed together and came up with a change management plan to **mitigate the team's uncertainties**. They drafted change communications to explain the change purpose and benefits, which would come from the leadership team. They collaborated to determine how each individual's responsibilities would change and emotionally reassure each person about their role and importance to drive the transformation success. They met with the head of Learning and Development (L&D) to create new capability training to drive adoption of the new software. David introduced Abigail to the vendor's point of contact to create an FAQs link and confirm that change communications accurately captured the software's purpose and benefits.

These few **change management examples to mitigate uncertainties** demonstrate how trusted relationships, transparent change communications, and helpful resources help people shift *from* feeling *uncertain* to feeling important and confident about their ability to learn new skills and **adopt changes**.

I think Abigail and her team will be motivated to stay at the company and drive success of the transformation. Do you?

 INSIDER TIP

The more we understand the **"why" behind uncertainty**, the better equipped we are to mitigate uncertainties. If you feel alone in your uncertainties about an upcoming marketing transformation, well, that's a pretty crummy feeling. I mean, who wants to feel alone when some big change is happening?! When I explain the human chemistry of change (why we fear change...all the science stuff earlier in this chapter) in an approachable way, **people no longer feel alone**. They feel **included**, and part of the **community** navigating the challenge together. And, that's a good thing.

 ## KEY TAKEAWAYS

Let's summarize key takeaways about the **human chemistry of change** as they relate to marketing transformation change management:

1. We are all born to change, so we are all **capable** of adopting a marketing transformation.
2. Our brains interpret **change** as **uncertainty,** and uncertainty as an **error** to be fixed.
3. Effective change management **mitigates uncertainty associated with change**, so everyone can chill out and get comfortable with the change.

You now understand the **human chemistry of change** and how it relates to change management. You're ahead of most people out there, and we only just finished Chapter 2!

"Marketers are **masters of change."**

—Dina Shapiro

CHAPTER 3

MARKETERS ARE UNIQUELY QUALIFIED TO LEAD

How to Apply Your Marketing Talents

"The future belongs to those who learn more skills and combine them in creative ways."
—Robert Greene

 LEARNING OBJECTIVES

After reading this chapter, you will be able to recognize how your marketing skills, experience, and traits uniquely qualify you to lead change management for marketing transformations.

DEFINITION OF SKILLS, EXPERIENCE, AND TRAITS

You've probably heard the words "skills," "experience," and "traits" before. To make sure we're all on the same page, I'll paraphrase definitions from Merriam-Webster Dictionary:

- A **skill** is an ability you learn and perform competently.
- **Experience** is gained knowledge through direct participation.
- A **trait** is a distinguishing, inherited personal characteristic.

 ## HOW TO READ THE NEXT THREE SECTIONS

For each of the tables on the next three pages, read **one row at a time, from left to right**.

There is no rush. I suggest that after you read each row, close your eyes, breathe slowly and deeply, and count to five before reading the next row.

Don't worry, it's nothing bad! But this is some new thinking, so I suggest you take your time to take it all in.

These examples are intended to demonstrate and not be a complete list.

The third column, "Application to Change Management" includes highlights of best practices that will be covered in detail in chapters 5-12.

Let's check them out...

 **SKILLS**

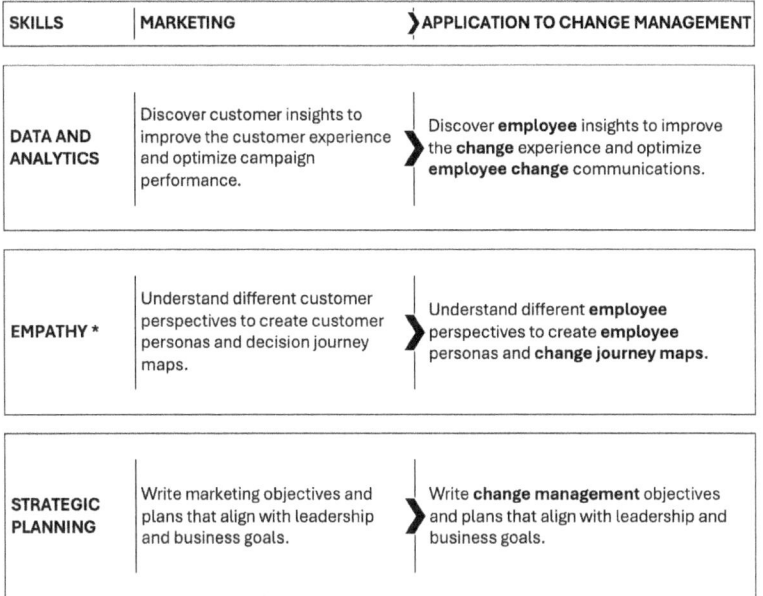

SKILLS	MARKETING	APPLICATION TO CHANGE MANAGEMENT
DATA AND ANALYTICS	Discover customer insights to improve the customer experience and optimize campaign performance.	Discover **employee** insights to improve the **change** experience and optimize **employee change** communications.
EMPATHY *	Understand different customer perspectives to create customer personas and decision journey maps.	Understand different **employee** perspectives to create **employee** personas and **change journey maps**.
STRATEGIC PLANNING	Write marketing objectives and plans that align with leadership and business goals.	Write **change management** objectives and plans that align with leadership and business goals.

*Some people define **empathy** as both a skill and trait. While I believe that some people are inherently more empathetic than others, I also believe that empathy **can be learned**, which is why I define it as a skill. In fact, Helen Riess, M.D., Founder, Chief Medical Officer, and Chairman of Empathetics, Inc. has developed **empathy training courses** based on the neuroscience of emotions for people to learn how to be more empathetic.

EXPERIENCE

EXPERIENCE*	MARKETING	➤ APPLICATION TO CHANGE MANAGEMENT
RELATIONSHIP MANAGEMENT	Collaborate with cross-discipline partners to create customer marketing communications, including internal such as Product Development and external such as agencies.	Collaborate with cross-discipline partners to create **employee change management communications,** including internal such as HR and external such as organizational change consultants.
LEADERSHIP	Inspire customers to try a new product or service and teach them how to do something differently, such as how they navigate a new mobile app.	**Inspire employees** to adopt a new technology such as a shared document site and train them how to navigate that new technology.
CRITICAL THINKING	Objectively analyze customer insights to write a Creative Brief that solves a consumer problem.	Objectively analyze **employee** insights to write a **Change Management Brief** to overcome **employee uncertainties.**

*Here I refer to "experience" as a **noun**. We'll talk about "experience" the verb later.

TRAITS

TRAITS	MARKETING	APPLICATION TO CHANGE MANAGEMENT
ADAPTABLE	Flexible, curious, lifelong learners who adapt to constant marketing changes, such as new digital touch points, organizational changes, and technologies.	The entire impacted team **adapts** to the marketing transformation; they don't just ask other people to change, they change themselves too!
RESILIENT	Overcome barriers such as budget reductions or a competitive product improvement through relevant, engaging customer communications and experiences.	**Overcome** barriers to **change** through relevant and engaging **employee** communications and experiences.
EQ (EMOTIONAL INTELLIGENCE)	Strong social skills, overcome challenges, and defuse conflicts to move the process forward with a customer-first mentality.	Strong social skills, overcome **barriers to change**, and **mitigate uncertainties** to move the process forward with an **employee-first** mentality.

APPLICATION OF WHAT WE HAVE LEARNED: *Applying Marketing Skills, Experience, and Traits to Change Management*

This is a case study about Jack, a Marketing Director at a payroll company, who learned how to apply his marketing skills, experience, and traits to change management.

Jack was in charge of the shift from manual to automated cloud-based marketing analytics software. The goal of this transformation was to reduce the time spent on manual tasks, to free up people's time for critical thinking. Jack wanted his team to focus more on interpreting data, discovering insights, and acting on those insights to create positive customer and business impact.

Jack was confident about managing the transformation itself, meaning, to get the new software up and running. He had great relationships with the cross-discipline team, including his marketing direct reports, IT, Legal, and Finance. Jack also engaged an executive sponsor to help with leadership approvals.

Intuitively, he knew that he needed some sort of change management to ensure the transformation's success. However, he **lacked confidence** about his **change management skills, experience, and traits** due to little exposure to this discipline. Although he displayed a confident exterior, **inside he felt unsure** about how to bring his team along on this transformation journey.

Jack took a step back. He paused for quiet, individual reflection. He **wrote a list** of his marketing skills, experience, and traits that he could harness and apply to lead change management for this marketing transformation.

Then, he reached out to Cynthia, the head of HR, and explained the transformation purpose and need for change management. Cynthia introduced Jack to Alex, who worked on her HR team and had previous work experience in change management. Alex shared ideas about change management processes and best practices.

The combination of Jack's individual reflection, writing down thoughts and ideas, and additional perspective from a change management practitioner, seriously **built his confidence** and helped him create his approach to change management.

Jack **applied his marketing research and empathy skills**. He started with an internal *listening tour*. He interviewed colleagues to share their uncertainties about the upcoming transformation. He did his best to create a psychologically safe environment with no judgments. He was *empathetic* and created a list of uncertainties he heard from people, that he would need to mitigate. He fielded an internal *survey* to learn about different employees' readiness for change. This survey garnered insights from people who felt more comfortable sharing feedback anonymously.

Jack **applied his critical thinking experience**. He *analyzed* all the insights to create categories of employees' uncertainties and *ideas* for how to overcome those uncertainties.

Jack **tapped into his EQ**. He *collaborated* with internal teams. He worked with HR and Internal Communications to create change communications that followed company standards and tone. He partnered with L&D to create engaging training for how to use the automated cloud-based marketing analytics software. He was *thoughtful* about 1:1 meetings with each person on his team. He shared his expectations of them about their freed-up time with less manual work, to focus more on interpreting data, discovering insights, and acting on those insights to create positive customer and business impact.

Despite the team's uncertainties when they first heard about the new software launch, Jack effectively **applied his marketing skills, experience, and traits** to create a change management plan including relevant change communications and experiences to alleviate people's uncertainties and engage them to adopt the new software. With more time for critical thinking, the team was now able to identify both short- and long-term ideas to identify customer opportunities and build the business.

 **INSIDER TIP**

Change management skills, experience, and traits are critical to grow your business and **your career.** The Association of National Advertisers (ANA), a leading U.S. advertising and marketing trade association, published "The Marketing Capabilities Framework" study. The goal of this first-of-its-kind analysis was to elevate modern marketing talent to drive their organization's growth. Across the five modern growth-driving marketing archetypes identified, keywords relevant to change management include: **leader, transformation, visionary, influential, resilient, problem solver, empathetic, EQ, cross-functional collaborator,** and **adaptability.** *This demonstrates the importance of having change management skills, experience, and traits in your repertoire/profile/resumé/CV/bio if you wish to drive your organization's growth and advance in your marketing career.*

KEY TAKEAWAYS

Let's summarize key takeaways about why marketers (yes, you, my brilliant marketers) are uniquely qualified to lead marketing transformation change management:

1. Marketers have a **unique combination** of skills, experience, and traits to lead change management for marketing transformations.
2. **Every marketer,** at any level or tenure in an organization, has the ability to lead, advocate, or participate in marketing transformation change initiatives.
3. If you want to be a successful marketer today, and in the future, **change leadership and transformation must be in your repertoire.**

In the next chapter, I will demonstrate how everyone benefits when marketers take the lead on change management for marketing transformations.

*"It's time to **change how change is managed** for marketing transformations."*

—Dina Shapiro

CHAPTER 4

WHAT HAPPENS WHEN MARKETERS LEAD:

Everyone Benefits!

"The quality of your life is the quality of your relationships."
—Tony Robbins

 LEARNING OBJECTIVES

After reading this chapter, you will be able to recognize why marketers should lead change management for marketing transformations and what people look for in those who lead.

REMINDER

I am **not** saying...

> ...that marketers should lead **every** change management initiative across the entire organization (i.e., do not attempt to tackle *every* slice in the entire organization-wide change management pizza pie).

I **am** saying...

> ...that marketers should lead change management specifically for **marketing transformations** (i.e., just that *one* slice of the change management pizza pie).

 WHY MARKETERS SHOULD TAKE THE LEAD

You may be thinking:

"Whoa! Stop! I already have so much work! Why would I want to take on even more work?!"

~ or ~

"Aren't there *other* people who should lead change management?"

Yes, marketers already have tons of work on their plate. I've been there. I get it.

But **no**, marketers should **not** delegate marketing transformation change management to others. Here's why:

1. As we established in Chapter 1, according to multiple credible sources over several decades, **only 1/3 of transformations succeed.**

2. Among marketers working in organizations currently undergoing change management, **only 48% are satisfied** with the change management impact.
3. 52% of marketers feel that there is **poor leadership** from those leading change efforts.
4. 46% of marketers claim a **lack of employee feedback** during changes.
5. 87% of marketers agree that change **without change management** is likely to **fail**.

Source for #2-5 above: Gartner (What can I say? I'm a fan.)

I am **not**...

... disparaging people or disciplines who currently lead or work in change management.

I **am**...

...highlighting that **most marketers feel that current change management initiatives are not working well**.

Have you heard the saying, credited to Albert Einstein, *"Insanity is doing the same thing over and over again and expecting different results"*?

It is time to **change how change is managed** for marketing transformations.

BENEFITS WHEN MARKETERS TAKE THE LEAD

When marketers lead change management for marketing transformations, everyone benefits.

Why?

Because, as we established in the previous chapter, marketers have amazing skills, experience, and traits to harness in change management! Yes, I am talking to you, my brilliant marketers.

I asked seven of my favorite Fortune 500 CMOs who they think should lead change management for marketing transformations. Here's what they said:

- *"Of course, marketers should do this! They do this for a living! They sell. It's marketing. They are marketing the change and actions people need to take."*

- *"The work needs to get done and managed closer to where the change is happening. You need that person who is implementing the change to be involved."*

- *"Marketing should lead because we have the vision, but we need CEO and sales support."* (Hang tight, we'll talk about those stakeholders later.)

- *"This is like a special assignment, so put together your SWAT team, those who are pulled out of the day-to-day, the high potentials, and task them with delivering the change."*

- *"Others such as HR or consultants can help with templates or the process, but marketers must lead this."*

- *"I think it must be the marketers who lead the change management for marketing transformation, even if they use or collaborate with the external consultant. They can communicate what we are doing, why, etc. because this is part of their job to begin with. The buck stops with them. External consultants cannot be front and center of that. Marketers have skin in the game. It's for their team and very much about helping them succeed. And yes, marketers know how to do this; they understand the audience, communicate the benefit, and know how to engage."*

- *"Needs to be a marketer who is an experienced leader with credibility in marketing who knows you and gets you. HR can help sensitize the leaders to the human dimensions of the challenge that they will encounter, but the message needs to be delivered by someone who understands the impact that this will have on us."*

I hope those quotes build your confidence to lead change management for marketing transformations!

But wait, here are even more **benefits** and reasons for marketers to take the lead....

Marketers create engaging customer experiences so they can create **engaging employee transformation experiences**.

Marketers create insightful customer personas and decision journey maps to personalize customer communications so they can create **insightful employee personas and Change Journey Maps to personalize employee change communications**.

Marketers are (or soon will be) **subject matter experts** (SMEs) of the marketing transformation itself so they can explain the transformation details in a **P**ragmatic, **S**imple, and **P**ainless way (what I call PSP, more about this later).

Marketers consistently **navigate change throughout their careers**, such as new CMOs who join the team, budget cuts, new digital touch points, and new technology like AI, so they are **empathetic** with their colleagues who are experiencing change.

Remember our definition of change management for marketing transformations?

Change management is a process to **advocate for the human side** of a marketing transformation.

As a Chief Brand Strategy Officer from a global technology company shared with me:

> "People must recognize that the change management is more important than the marketing transformation itself. People say they love change, but they don't want to change. They want others to change but not themselves. We need marketing leaders who get it and will participate in the transformation, whether it's the good, bad, or ugly."

Because marketers have navigated changes since the beginning of their careers, they **empathize** with others who need to adopt changes. Marketers are excellent **advocates of change** because they have experienced so many changes themselves. They are on your side. They hear you. They feel you.

 LEADERSHIP QUALITIES PEOPLE SEEK

Here's what executives tell me they look for in marketers to lead change management for marketing transformations:

- *"Stature"*
- *"Empathy"*
- *"Have a vision"*
- *"Well-respected"*

- *"Engage the right talent"*
- *"Can bring everyone along"*
- *"Strong leadership skills"*
- *"Aptitude to be tactical and deliver"*
- *"Someone who can create a safe space"*
- *"Courage of conviction to make things happen"*
- *"Change management is an art and a science. It's all about understanding."*
- *"Understand the problem that needs to be solved and the challenges leading up to this point."*
- *"Need left-brain methodology to analyze and make decisions, need right brain to empathize and be creative."*

Do you see yourself in any points above? Even one? Yes? Then you're on the right track!

 ## APPLICATION OF WHAT WE HAVE LEARNED: *Recognizing The Benefits When Marketers Lead Change Management*

This is a case study about Isabella, a Senior Marketer Manager at a homebuilding company, who *unexpectedly* took the reigns on change management for a new marketing technology.

Isabella's supervisor told her that IT was evaluating technology vendors to integrate customer data across multiple disciplines. The objective was to improve the customer experience and democratize the data, to make the same data accessible to the cross-discipline team.

She felt **uncertain** about what this change would mean for her and which **other disciplines** to include in this transformation. Isabella spoke with her colleagues to understand their concerns and questions. She had no specific experience in change management, but her **marketing skills, experience, and traits kicked in.**

She suggested to her supervisor that they create internal communications for departments affected by this change. Isabella used her experience in customer communications to write the **change story.** She used the PSP approach, to explain in a **P**ragmatic, **S**imple, and **P**ainless way, how the technology works, the benefits, and expectations of all stakeholders involved to adopt the new technology.

Isabella's change story included an overview of the technology vendors under consideration, vendor capabilities, objectives, and benefits. She clearly **communicated benefits** such as data integration, internal data transparency and accessibility, and the ability to collaborate internally to optimize the customer experience. She explained that consolidating with one vendor would save money over the long term. She **reassured** people that they would spend less time finding data due to the integration, which would free up their time for deeper analysis, critical thinking, and uncovering relevant, actionable customer insights.

Isabella used her market research skills to write a **survey** to find out how her colleagues felt before versus after her communications.

The **entire team benefited** from Isabella taking the lead on change management for their marketing transformation. The survey feedback after the technology launch was stellar. 97% of her colleagues said that they felt *"respected," "included,"* and *"comfortable"* understanding the change, its purpose and benefits, and how they would be impacted.

INSIDER TIP

Change management expertise is in demand! According to Business Talent Group (BTG), a Heidrick & Struggles company, a premier executive search consultant that works with more than 70% of Fortune 1000 companies across sectors and industries, **leaders are seeking talent to assist with change management (up +26%)**, and **change management is the #1 in-demand skill for transformation initiatives.**

 KEY TAKEAWAYS

Let's summarize key takeaways about why everyone benefits when marketers lead marketing transformation change management:

1. It is time to **change how change is managed** for marketing transformations.
2. Marketers are **best qualified** to lead marketing transformation change management.
3. Change management for transformations is a **top skill** desired by leadership.

You now understand your opportunity and power to modify how change is managed for marketing transformations. The rest of this book explains **how** to lead marketing transformation change management in a unique way. These are the "how" details that I promised you earlier, which people have started referring to as *Shapiro's CMfM (Change Management for Marketers)*.

*"Personas build an **emotional bond** with employees throughout their change journey."*

—Dina Shapiro

CHAPTER 5

EMPLOYEE PERSONAS

How to Personalize Change Communications

"Clients do not come first. Employees come first.If you take care of your employees, they will take care of the clients."
—Sir Richard Branson

 LEARNING OBJECTIVES

After reading this chapter, you will be able to define an employee persona, describe its benefits and role in your change management plan, and write an employee persona.

 EMPLOYEE PERSONA DEFINITION

An employee persona is:

A research-based, fictional profile of your employees' demographics, motivations, expectations, attitudes, and behaviors, including decision criteria you must address for employees to adopt and sustain the marketing transformation.

Let's break down that definition.

Research-based: This is key. I can't tell you how often I see generic, pre-defined, or made-up employee personas. Let's apply our marketing experience from writing *customer* personas. If someone said to you, "There are generic, pre-defined customer personas that I made up for you that apply to every type of industry, business, brand, product and service," would you, my brilliant marketer, accept that? No, you would not! Just like you write research-based, customer personas *specific* to *your* business, brand, product, or service, you also need to write **customized employee personas** specific to your marketing transformation change management.

Fictional: An employee persona is **representative** of a particular group or segment of employees. It is not intended to represent only one actual person. This is like how customer personas in marketing represent a segment of people and not one specific real person.

Demographics: Statistical characteristics to define a segment of the population, such as age, ethnicity, household income, and marital status. Demographics are necessary and helpful to create *customer* campaigns and media plans. However, for *internal employee* communications, we can think of demographics more like a **discipline** or department, **tenure** at the organization, or organizational **seniority** or **level**. Depending on the type of transformation and organizational culture, demographics may be optional in your employee persona template.

A word of caution if you do choose to include demographics: Be careful not to assume or discriminate. For example, please do not assume that because someone is in a certain age group, that they can or cannot do something or think in a particular way. Like, "old people don't get technology," or "young people feel entitled and are lazy." That's just plain wrong and unfair and will kill your change management initiative before you take the first step.

Motivations: The need, reason, willingness, enthusiasm, or incentive **to do something**. Examples include an employee who *lacks* motivation to change, or an employee who *is motivated* to change because they understand the marketing transformation benefits.

Expectations: A feeling, belief, or anticipation about **what will or should happen** in the future. Examples include employees who *fear* the transformation because their job may no longer be necessary or employees who *progress* in their career after they adopt the marketing transformation.

Attitudes: **Feelings, opinions, or mental positions** about something or someone, about a fact, state-of-mind, or manner. Examples include employees who have a *negative* attitude about adopting a marketing transformation or employees who have an *optimistic* attitude about the positive outcomes of the marketing transformation.

Behaviors: **How someone acts** or conducts themself, or their actions or responses to stimulation or their environment. Examples include employees who behave in a defiant manner to *reject* a transformation or employees who *adapt* to a transformation.

Decision criteria you must address for employees to adopt and sustain the marketing transformation: Decision criteria are conscious or subconscious **factors, categories, or standards** that employees use to judge if, why, or how they will adopt the marketing transformation. Decision criteria are a major **actionable** part of the employee persona definition because they get to the bottom line about **whether employees will or will not adopt** the marketing transformation. This is the big kahuna! (But often not included. Sigh.) Examples include employees who will adopt a change associated with a promotion or pay increase or if provided with new capability training.

Sources consulted for "motivations," "expectations," "attitudes," and "behaviors" paraphrased definitions above include Cambridge Dictionary and Merriam-Webster Dictionary.

BENEFITS AND THE ROLE OF EMPLOYEE PERSONAS

Here are my two favorite responses to the question: "Do you think we need employee personas for marketing transformation change management?"

- *"We need to identify and manage influential internal people who are negative and not supportive. Otherwise, it keeps feeling like one step forward and two steps backwards due to those couple of people. We need their buy-in."*

- *"Identify those in your organization, the people who really want to change. Then there's the group of people who would like to change but don't have the self-confidence. Then there's the group who just does not want to change. We end up putting lots of energy toward those first two groups because they are the most agile. The third group, well, they just like the status quo and are so scared. This is the hardest part to deal with. So we need to identify those groups; some people are who they are, and we need to help them navigate the transformation."*

Employee personas **drive success** in your change management plan by helping you **personalize** the employee change experience and change story. Different personas have different motivations, expectations, attitudes, behaviors, and decision criteria. Personalized, empathetic communications **vary** by the persona to create a relevant, engaging change experience.

Employee personas facilitate **internal coordination** and **overcome silos** because all change management stakeholders work off common language and understanding about each employee persona and how best to engage.

According to Gallup, a global analytics and advisory firm that helps clients create exceptional employee workplaces, **personalized internal communications build an emotional bond with employees**.

According to Gallup, Calm, and my consulting projects, benefits of this emotional bond include:

- Creating a sense of belonging
- Feeling more secure and supported

- Reducing stress and anxiety
- Opening lines of communication
- Facilitating dialogue
- Increasing employee retention and advocacy of the marketing transformation
- **Reducing feelings of uncertainty** (there's that word "uncertainty" again!)
- And, dare I say it, making time at work more **enjoyable**

 ## HOW TO WRITE AN EMPLOYEE PERSONA

If, based on the above information, you agree that employee personas are important, here are my **7 steps to write** an employee persona:

1. **Consult with your cross-discipline team.** Find out if anyone in the organization has experience writing employee personas. They can share their positive experiences, lessons learned, and valuable insight as you research and write your personas. Invite HR, other internal disciplines, or external change management consultants to share their thoughts and questions. The combination of these diverse, experienced perspectives will make the work better and help with leadership buy-in.

2. **Start thinking about your employee persona template.** What elements will you include? Consult our definition of "employee persona" above for inspiration. What information and insights will you need? It's okay if you don't have a final template at this point. But some direction will be helpful as you go ahead to step #3.

3. **Conduct internal research with employees**. Include a mix of anonymous and direct feedback formats. Focus groups or 1:1 interviews are good for those who are comfortable speaking up spontaneously. Observations are good for process or technology transformations. An anonymous online survey is good for those who wish to be more private or like more time to think. Think ahead to insights you will need to create your entire change management plan, including your employee personas, Change Journey Map, and Change Management Brief (more details in chapters 6-10). Think about all employee touch points at your disposal for research. For example, you can ask questions in an internal employee blog or talk with people informally at a Town Hall or company event. If the touch point is managed by another discipline or team, talk with the right people in advance so they understand what you wish to accomplish, and confirm if they are comfortable with you conducting research in that environment or format. Most importantly, stay objective! Try to avoid pre-dispositions going into the research. Be a good listener.

4. **Synthesize research insights with key takeaways**. Categorize and prioritize insights to inform how you write employee personas. Hold aside insights that will be relevant later to create your Change Journey Map and Change Management Brief (more about those in chapters 6-10).

5. **Complete your employee persona templates**. Remember, you will have multiple employee personas, not one employee persona. This work is hard! Set aside

thinking time to evaluate research insights with an open mind. Edit, edit, edit. Think about which points are best communicated with visuals or icons. Create a name for each employee persona. Go for names that are descriptive, specific, and memorable, like "Spectator Sam." Don't be afraid to have some fun with this! Consider a concise, catchy quote or headline to support the name and help describe each persona, like "Spectator Sam: Observes Before Doing." Share your draft employee persona templates with others for feedback. Be open to feedback. Remember that feedback is a gift. Revise, revise, revise. Balance robust and insightful with concise and readable. One page is ideal.

6. **Move forward with the approval process**. This varies by the organization. Include the right stakeholders for approval (details about those in chapters 11-12). Repeat a few steps from #5 above, such as to be open to feedback, edit, and remember that feedback is a gift :)

7. **Internally publish the approved employee persona templates**. Decide who specifically needs this information. Typically, this is not an organization-wide distribution. Not because it's a secret, but because this information is most helpful to a select few and not relevant to others.

Clients ask me, "*How many employee personas should we have?*" There is no magic number. Typically, three to four personas account for the majority of total employees. However, depending on the size and complexity of your business and transformation, you could have more.

Remember that **each employee persona should be distinct** to create distinct change stories or change experiences. If you have two personas that feel similar, for example, you have the same change story and provide the same training, perhaps it's better to combine those two personas to one persona.

 ## APPLICATION OF WHAT WE HAVE LEARNED: *Writing An Employee Persona*

This is a case study about Ariel, a Marketing Director for an airline, who created employee personas.

Ariel's CMO was leading the launch of a cloud-based software to **personalize** the customer experience. Ariel was asked to create **employee personas** for the change management plan, to help the internal team adopt this new technology.

Ariel understood the **importance** of employee personas to **personalize** internal change story communications, because it's *similar* to creating customer personas to personalize external marketing communications.

This was Ariel's first time writing employee personas, so she was kind of nervous. She had a close relationship with her agency strategic planner, Harry, with whom she collaborated to augment her own marketing skills, experience, and traits.

There was no established employee persona template, so they created a template including motivations, expectations, attitudes, and behaviors. Ariel shared this template with the cross-discipline team. A few people suggested that she add one item, decision criteria, to the template. She made that change, reviewed it with her CMO, and gained approval of her template.

Here's where Ariel landed on her employee persona template:

PERSONA NAME:	
MOTIVATIONS ▶	
EXPECTATIONS ▶	
ATTITUDES ▶	
BEHAVIORS ▶	
DECISION CRITERIA ▶	

Next came the really hard part! How many personas? How to complete each template with insights for each persona? Ariel had limited time and resources, and although she was still kind of nervous about the process, she was quickly gaining confidence. She kept going back to which of her marketing best practices she could apply to create personas.

She created a list of internal people across levels and disciplines who would be impacted by this marketing transformation. Working alongside Harry, her agency Strategic Planner, they wrote the research guide and questionnaire. She quickly moderated three focus groups, interviewed seven executives 1:1, and invited an additional 135 people to complete an anonymous survey. Ariel also had informal chats with random people at the quarterly Town Hall to gather more insights.

Ariel and Harry were quite a team! They summarized research insights in an interesting, creative way. They wrote one page of highlights and included back up pages with details and anonymous quotes to bring the research findings, insights, and recommendations to life.

Next, they had to fill in the blanks in the template, and for multiple employee personas. No small feat! They decided to have an all-day team meeting to work on each persona together. They had a great meeting but were far from finished. It took one more all-day meeting for the team to agree to four employee personas.

Ariel shared the research insights, recommendations, and four employee personas with the cross-discipline team. She actively listened to their questions and answered non-defensively. After receiving their feedback, Ariel made a few revisions.

Finally! Their research, astute marketing brains, perseverance, and ideas from the team suggested these four personas:

1. *"Pioneer Pam,"* a technology lover and early adopter
2. *"Check-in Cathy,"* who likes to check with her colleagues before deciding how she feels
3. *"Questioning Quentin,"* who is uncertain about new technology and avoids it
4. *"Ambassador Andrew,"* who advocates for new technologies that have been positive experiences

Ariel shared insights and recommendations with her CMO, who then socialized with her peers, the company's C-Suite.

Minimal revisions were suggested, which Ariel completed. She was super excited to move forward.

Let's take a look at one persona, "Pioneer Pam" below.*

PIONEER PAM A technology lover and early adopter	
MOTIVATIONS	Willing and motivated to adopt the new technology. She may not yet know the specific benefits but is an enthusiastic believer that new technology improves effectiveness and efficiency.
EXPECTATIONS	Expects to progress in her career after adopting the marketing technology. She will work better and faster to grow customer relationships.
ATTITUDES	Feels optimistic about the positive outcomes of the marketing transformation because she trusts the CMO and IT team to bring in new relevant technologies.
BEHAVIORS	Quick to adapt to a marketing transformation that's technologically driven and facilitates more personalization in customer communications and experiences.
DECISION CRITERIA	Despite her trust in the company's leadership and IT team, she will only adopt the change if provided with new capability training, use cases as more and more people adopt the technology, and an open feedback loop to share and hear about others' experiences.

*This is an abbreviated example for demonstration. This book has size and color limitations. When you create your persona, I recommend:

- Using colors, icons, and other visuals to make the persona engaging and bring the persona to life.
- Including all elements of the persona on one page.

How did Ariel use all four personas? Interested to hear more? We'll continue Ariel's story in chapters 6-10 as we see how personas were used to build out the Change Journey Map including stages, messaging, and touch points, and the Change Management Brief. Stay with me.

INSIDER TIP

When conducting employee research, **ask people to complain** to focus on their **problem**. People can articulate problems more easily than solutions. (I learned this research best practice while working at BBDO, which will always be my favorite agency in the world.) For example, someone can easily express unhappiness due to a lack of information and training. Once you hear that problem, it's your job as the change manager to think of solutions, such as creating in-person workshops, asynchronous/on-demand online training, and train-the-trainer materials for supervisors to cover training topics for a smaller team.

 KEY TAKEAWAYS

Let's summarize key takeaways about creating insightful employee personas to personalize communications:

1. An employee persona is a **research-based fictional profile** of your employees' motivations, expectations, attitudes, behaviors, and decision criteria.
2. Employee personas help you create **personalized** change experiences and communications.
3. Personalized change experiences create an **emotional bond** between leadership, change agents, and employees to drive marketing transformation **adoption** and **sustainability.**

In the next few chapters, we'll cover how to use your employee personas to inform your Employee Change Journey Map and Change Management Brief. Let's read on.

*"I know everyone wants it to be over, but change management is **never really over.**"*

—Dina Shapiro

CHAPTER 6

THE EMPLOYEE CHANGE JOURNEY

Map Out the Ride and the Destination

*"Attaining lasting happiness requires that we enjoy
the journey on our way toward a destination we
deem valuable. Happiness is not about making it
to the peak of the mountain nor is it about climbing
aimlessly around the mountain; happiness is the
experience of climbing toward the peak."*

—Tal Ben-Shahar

 LEARNING OBJECTIVES

After reading this chapter, you will be able to define an
Employee Change Journey Map and micro-moments,
recognize their roles and benefits, and create an Employee
Change Journey Map template.

🔍 EMPLOYEE CHANGE JOURNEY MAP DEFINITION

An Employee Change Journey Map is:

A visual framework that articulates the mindset and behaviors of employees as they experience changes throughout a marketing transformation.

Let's break down that definition:

Framework: I'll paraphrase this definition from Cambridge Dictionary and Merriam-Webster Dictionary. A framework is a **conceptual structure** of ideas and information that is used to build or plan something, such as a map.

Mindset and behaviors of employees as they experience changes: We create our journey map from the **employee perspective.** Remember our change management definition from Chapter 1: Change management is a process to advocate for the **human** side of a marketing transformation. Our Change Journey Map should have an **employee-first** perspective.

Throughout: I had a painful, lengthy conversation with myself about "throughout" versus "through." Here's where I landed. "Through" suggests a start point and an end point. **"Throughout"** suggests an **entire cycle** of a marketing transformation. This is a critical distinction. Many marketers say things like this to me: "*I just want the transformation to be over! When will this f*@^k%#g thing end?!?*" I understand the emotional need for the transformation to have an end point. Here comes the "but" part. *But,* marketing transformations tend to be more cyclical than linear. (People don't like it too much when I say that. Hang tight. More about "linear" and "cyclical" in the next chapter.)

A QUICK SIDEBAR: OTHER TYPES OF EMPLOYEE JOURNEY MAPS

You may have heard of an **Employee Lifecycle** or **Employee Journey,** typically owned by HR or Leadership, which are **different** from an **Employee Change Journey** (discussed above and in the next few chapters).

An **Employee Lifecycle** or **Employee Journey** tracks the stages and experiences of an employee starting as a prospective employee, through interviewing, hiring, onboarding, engagement, performance reviews, recognition, career planning, and exiting.

An **Employee Change Journey Map** is specific to stages and experiences throughout a **distinct change within** the employee's lifecycle, a **marketing transformation** (our focus in this book).

If your organization has an established Employee Lifecycle or Employee Journey, your **Employee Change Journey** should **align** with or **support** that framework as appropriate. This is a good example of when to collaborate with an internal stakeholder such as HR or an external consultant that helps with your company's organizational management.

BENEFITS AND THE ROLE OF AN EMPLOYEE CHANGE JOURNEY MAP

An Employee Change Journey Map requires thinking **from the employee's perspective**. What are their **uncertainties** and why? What do they **think, need**, and **feel**? What are their choices and behaviors? What information and experience will help them **navigate** a marketing transformation to adopt and sustain the change?

Enter: **micro-moments.**

You may be familiar with micro-moments in the context of customers (i.e., customer micro-moments in a customer decision journey). It's similar with employees. **Employee micro-moments are intent-rich moments when they learn, go, do, or buy something relating to the marketing transformation.** Some examples:

- **Learn** about the purpose and benefits of the marketing transformation.
- **Go** to interactive Town Halls to ask questions about the marketing transformation and hear real time responses.
- **Do** advocate to colleagues about how the transformation has helped them do their job better in less time.
- **Buy** into and choose to adopt the marketing transformation (so this is more of a conceptual "buy" versus when a customer trades money to buy a product or service).

An insight-driven Employee Change Journey Map recognizes and incorporates employee micro-moments, so you can engage them **when, where, and how they want.**

An Employee Change Journey Map also aligns the organization about the employee change experience.

Ultimately, this all improves the change experience to drive employee **retention, loyalty** and **advocacy**, which (wink, wink) **aligns** with HR's Employee Lifecycle or Employee Journey.

HOW TO WRITE AN EMPLOYEE CHANGE JOURNEY MAP TEMPLATE

If you agree that an Employee Change Journey Map drives success of change management of your marketing transformation, here are my six tips to create your template:

1. **One page.** Less is more. Most people don't like to write or read anything super lengthy. Make your template readable, manageable, and engaging. Your Employee Change Journey Map should be a one-page snapshot.

2. **Persona**. Include highlights from your full-page persona. Every organization has multiple personas, about different groups of employees, that experience change differently.

3. **Stages**. A change journey stage is each step or phase in the persona's change journey. Each stage should be written in colloquial language from the persona's perspective.

4. **Messaging**. This is the information you share with the persona about the change and what the change means for them.

5. **Touch points**. Change journey touch points are the internal environments or places in which the communications and dialogue occur with each persona.

6. **Include visuals.** It is more engaging and easier to understand a **visual** journey map. Leave sufficient space within the visual template to fill in information

and insights for points #3-5 above. You can research online for visual map template ideas. This step is key and typically takes more time than people expect. Your map most likely should be cyclical, not a straight line (more about this in the next chapter, I promise).

The list above represents **foundational** items to include in a **starter** Employee Change Journey Map. We'll get into more details, examples, and "how-to" tips for points #3-5 above in the next few chapters.

Over time, I encourage you to:

- Add **more items that are relevant** to your industry, organizational culture, and marketing transformation specifics.

- **Optimize your map template** to include more insights and information you gather. As you lead more change management initiatives for more marketing transformations, you will gain the confidence and experience to optimize your map template over time.

- **Research** other templates online for ideas to build on your starter template when you are ready.

- **"Don't try to boil the ocean."** Hearing other people's feedback and seeing other examples out there may tempt you to add in lots of information in your template. At least for your first project, I recommend sticking to the foundational best practices (points #1-6 that I shared above). You can evolve to a more advanced template map later.

Remember that you will use the **same template** for each persona's Change Journey Map; however, you **fill in the template differently for each distinct persona**. Each employee persona has **their own Change Journey Map**.

Why? Because different personas navigate the marketing transformation differently.

So if you have *four* employee personas, you will need to complete *four* different Employee Change Journey Maps using the same template. Some people may tell you that there is only one Employee Change Journey Map. If that was the case, what would be the point of multiple employee personas? And how would you customize the experience for each persona with the same Change Journey Map?

 APPLICATION OF WHAT WE HAVE LEARNED: *Designing Your Change Journey Map Framework*

You met Ariel, the Marketing Director of an airline in our last chapter. She has been working on **change management** for the launch of a cloud-based software to personalize the customer experience. You may recall me referring to her CMO.

Enter: Oliver, her CMO.

Oliver has been with the company for 18 months. Previously, he held a variety of senior marketing positions at three other companies. Oliver is one of the few marketers who has experience leading successful change management initiatives for marketing transformations at other companies.

While he is glad that the team buys into the concept of employee personas, he is not convinced that they understand the broader context of the Employee Change Journey Map. Oliver knew that **education** and **inspiration** were needed to move the process forward with the team's buy-in.

At the next team meeting, he defined a Change Journey Map, a **visual framework to empathize** with the employee perspective as they progress through a marketing transformation. He explained the **benefits**, for example, understanding people's uncertainties so they can be resolved, and what they **think, need,** and **feel** so change management can help them navigate the transformation with less pain and in less time. Oliver also discussed employee **micro-moments**, which help engage people **when, where, and how they want.** He compared employee and customer micro-moments for context. People started to head nod and understand the role of an employee Change Journey Map.

Oliver asked the team if they would like him to lead a workshop to ideate employee micro-moments for one persona. Then the team would get more comfortable working among themselves to ideate micro-moments for other personas. He explained that micro-moment insights would help the team create a Change Journey Map for each persona, and that would be the next workshop he would facilitate.

Fast forward to three weeks later. Oliver and team completed the workshop with rave reviews. People were engaged and excited to move forward and build out Change Journey Maps.

We will continue this story in the next chapter. I'll share the change journey framework and stages created by the team for one of the personas, "Pioneer Pam."

INSIDER TIP

Some people ask me about external consultants or internal colleagues with change management certifications or certificates, and how to work with them. If you are required to follow a specific change management approach or point of view, or use a particular template, there is no need to argue. If you feel comfortable sharing a different point of view, do so with solid rationale (feel free to cite anything from this book). But **don't fall on a sword or damage your reputation or relationships unnecessarily**. Do your best to adapt to the required process and include select highlights from points #1-6 above and other specifics that you'll read in this book's remaining chapters.

 KEY TAKEAWAYS

Let's summarize key takeaways about the Employee Change Journey Map:

1. An Employee Change Journey Map is a visual framework that articulates the **mindset** and **behaviors** of employees as they experience **changes** throughout a marketing transformation.
2. A key benefit of an Employee Change Journey Map is to improve employee **relevance** by engaging people how, where, and when they want.
3. A **starter** template for an Employee Change Journey Map includes a persona, stages, touch points, and messaging.

In our next three chapters, I will share best practices and tips for how to complete your Employee Change Journey Map with robust, actionable insights. Let's go!

*"Bring people in **early** and **nurture** the relationship to build trust and credibility."*

—Dina Shapiro

CHAPTER 7

CHANGE JOURNEY STAGES

Engage Employees Early and Keep That Relationship Going

"One step at a time is all it takes to get you there."
—Emily Dickinson

 LEARNING OBJECTIVES

After reading this chapter, you will be able to define a change journey stage, recognize its role and importance, and write stages from the employee perspective.

 CHANGE JOURNEY STAGES DEFINITION

Employee change journey stages are:

The sequence of a persona's mindsets and behaviors during their change experience.

Let's break down that definition:

Stage: Some people may view the words "stage" and "phase" as synonymous or use one word to define the other. For marketing transformation change management, they are quite different.

A stage **progresses** whereas a phase can **end.** *Stages* are different and separate periods of development within the overall marketing transformation and can be used to predict what an employee likely will experience next. A *phase* is more like a period of behavior that may stop after a while, like when a 2-year-old child goes through a "tantrum phase," though I've been told that some adults can do this too, ha ha ha.

Effective change management is when an employee **progresses** through their change journey to adopt and sustain the marketing transformation. Change *mismanagement* is when an employee gets *stuck* in the beginning or middle phase of their change journey and does not adapt to the marketing transformation.

Sequence: To paraphrase from Cambridge Dictionary and Merriam-Webster Dictionary, a sequence is a series of related events linked together in a particular order related to a cause. Change journey stages should **flow from one to the next** and **relate** to each other in an **integrated** way.

Employee/Persona: Our emphasis must always be on the employee, the **human** side of the transformation. How does the person feel? What does the person not understand? What are the person's uncertainties? Including the word "employee" in our definition reminds us to keep our **people** at the **heart** of the transformation.

Mindsets and behaviors: As we discussed in Chapter 5, a mindset includes motivations, expectations, or attitudes. Behaviors are how someone acts or responds.

Change: Well, a change is pretty much anything that's different from what it used to be for an employee. A change that may seem small to one person, may seem big to another person. Remember that different people are impacted by change in different ways.

Experience: We defined this word in Chapter 3 when we discussed marketers' skills, traits, and experience applicable to leading change management. In that chapter, we used the word "experience" as a noun, to "gain knowledge from direct participation." Here, I will define the word "experience" as a *verb*. To paraphrase from Cambridge Dictionary and Merriam-Webster Dictionary, experience is having been **affected through direct observation or participation**. So basically, it's when something happens to an employee that affects how they feel.

 ## BENEFITS AND THE ROLE OF CHANGE JOURNEY STAGES

Change journey stages provide **insight** into each **persona's mindsets and behaviors** and how we can help them through the transformation. What are they thinking? What do they need? What can we solve for them?

Understanding how an employee persona **naturally progresses** through a transformation provides valuable and necessary insight to create your change management plan.

Change journey stages **align** stakeholders about the employee journey to make the approval process smoother, faster, and easier.

Change journey stages are a **springboard** from which to write internal communication messaging and choose internal touch points (more about each of those in the next two chapters) to engage each persona when, where, and how they would like.

 HOW TO WRITE CHANGE JOURNEY STAGES

Here, we return to our Employee Change Journey Map template and start filling in blank spaces, starting with **stages**. Here are my eight steps to write Employee Change Journey stages:

1. **Write from the employee's perspective.** Review your research insights and persona (see Chapter 5) to write stages from the employee's point of view. Read the research verbatims, numbers, and insights with a fresh set of eyes and open mind. What does your research tell you about how this persona will progress through their change journey? Go back to your **employee micro-moments** to inform how you write stages.

2. **Identify employee moments of truth.** A moment of truth is when something **meaningful** happens and an **impression** is formed, or a **decision** is made that affects the **next stage** in the employee's change journey. A moment of truth could be when *information* is provided about the transformation, during an *interaction* such as capability training for the transformation, or a *conversation* about benefits or implications of a transformation. A moment of truth

can be positive or negative; in most cases, you'll have a mix of both.

3. **Keep it real.** Use language that is colloquial, relatable, and understandable. Avoid marketing lingo, jargon, or any words that turn people off or that they must look up the definition. Do not use words that make someone think, "Huh? What's that supposed to mean?" and start searching for definitions on their phone.

4. **Connect emotionally.** Journey stages are not the specific language that you use in employee communications. However, they do **set the tone** for those communications. Define stages with emotional language that's memorable and pulls people in, such as to "**Discover**" people's uncertainties and problems, or to "**Imagine**" new ways to improve the transformation or change management in the future.

5. **Start early.** Engage people early by identifying the *earliest moment or trigger* in their change journey. The earlier you share information about the transformation, the better, even if it's preliminary or incomplete. **Transparency** early on is key to build trust. As one CMO shared with me, "*Invite people in to partake in the transformation; don't try to just tell them to do it, you have to engage them early.*" Examples of an early stage from the employee's perspective are to feel **"Uninformed"** about the transformation purpose and benefits or **"Neglected"** when not consulted and included in the process.

6. **Don't leave people out in the cold.** Continue engagement to *sustain* the transformation; do not

disappear after the transformation launches and people initially adopt the change. Realistically, there will be problems to fix or ideas to improve the transformation itself or the change management. Let's say your organization launches new marketing technology. Continue helping people through the entire transformation from the initial launch, through training, feedback, and future technology updates or additions. Examples of stages after the launch of the transformation are to **"Sustain"** the excitement of the change or to request **"Feedback"** about desired improvements.

7. **Create one map of stages for each persona.** Remember that each persona has its own distinct Change Journey Map with its own change journey stages.

8. **Linear or cyclical?** Decide whether your persona's change journey is linear or cyclical.

Here's what's similar: Both linear and cyclical frameworks represent the **sequence** of a persona's **mindsets** and **behaviors** during the change experience.

But here's how they are different:

Linear change journey stages follow each other in a **line** with clear **start** and **end** points. Some people use **linear** change journey stages because they are:

- Viewed as predictable
- Appropriate for simple changes
- Perceived to be established frameworks
- Faster to align stakeholders

Examples of linear types of change journey models include Lewin, Kotter, and Prosci.

In my research and experience, there is limited support for linear, which focuses mostly on wanting the transformation and change management to be over, such as, *"I dread this being never-ending."* Or as another marketer explained:

"A cycle reminds me of a hamster wheel and is susceptible to burnout or heightened skepticism because it never ends, and it feels like here's yet another one. While there may be enterprise learning that comes from that and some squishy justification that we are training our people to be agile or athletes in change, that seldom happens. Like, people do not become in love with change because it happens all the time. Rather, they become frustrated with the never-ending-ness of changes and the theoretical benefit does not materialize. So you have active blockers, un-enthusiastic participants. I do not know about linear but believe that time-based, predictable steps, endpoints, evaluation points, reconciliations, conclusions and milestones are helpful. Plus, it helps to say, here is what worked, and these are the outcomes, but we also learned what did not work and now we'll address this thing, so people see the responsiveness but need to see cause-effect-outcome in a predicted fashion."

Cyclical change journey stages follow each other in a **circle** and **repeat** in the same or similar order. Some people use **cyclical** change journey stages because they are:

- Adaptable for complex transformations that require experimentation and learning

- More inclusive of human emotions
- An iterative feedback loop with refinements to achieve the desired change
- Flexible and collaborative to respond to changing situations and needs

Examples of cyclical types of change journey models include Burke-Litwin and PDCA.

People reluctantly lean toward the cyclical approach, such as unenthusiastically saying, *"In reality, it is cyclical."* Here's what a few more marketers say about it:

- *"If the transformation is mar-tech, there will always be updates and improvements, so the change never really ends."*

- *"In a perfect world, it would be a cycle; bring everyone along, continue to go through with updates or add more functionality."*

- *"For marketing, it must be cyclical. So much of it is test and learn. It's insane to tell someone, 'Here's how to do this,' we must all look forward, try things and experiment."*

- *"People think they are done, like with a* (vendor name redacted) *implementation, but no, the system must continue to evolve to align with business changes and technological updates."*

- *"When do you know when change management is done, when is it finished? It's not linear, but yes, it's cyclical. But how does this not become an endless journey without ever reaching the end goal? What are the metrics of success for this—in terms of application, implementation and goals achieved? Such as budget saved, processes efficiencies, etc. Marketers can get distracted. How do you talk about this in terms the rest of the C-suite can understand and respect—that are not vanity metrics—to make a noticeable shift to executives and sponsors and leadership."*

- *"I can see it as being cyclical across the organization that there is always a need for change. I always want to think of these as a big giant unwieldy project that happens once; it's linear, and it's done. It's like if you re-architect your house, which happens once, but you might have a deep clean or refresh your furniture. The one big ugly beast you start, and it's done and if it's done correctly, then you anticipate the needs for 5-10 years out. So the 20-point step now becomes the 10-point step, like to add a garage but don't build a whole new house."*

I really don't want to complicate things here, but in the spirit of sharing, some people answer "*neither*" to the linear vs. cyclical question. Here's what they have to say about it:

- *"It's like a string of spaghetti."*

- *"I don't see it as cyclical, but I do see it as bite-size pieces. There's an overarching roadmap. People will start with phases, like MVP, then phase 2, and so on."*

- *"Ugh, it's like a swarm of bees when it's not managed properly. People go back and forth based on their personal needs or opinions, or depending on what their manager thinks, or what's happening around them. If even just one person loses a supervisor or vice versa, the entire team can be in a new, different place."*

- *"I don't see it as linear. I think of it more like a lattice, like a puzzle, because not every aspect of marketing will change at the same time, maybe different work streams and each has its own change management piece. Always look to see how it all fits together and sequence to get to the end goal. Understand inter-dependencies of the change and what does that mean for the timing, etc. Test and learn and inform. Think about it as this matrix of activities and how do you keep playing chess and what are your moves and based on data do you need to pivot on one piece but keep moving on other aspects of that change?"*

9. **Conventional or customized?** Decide whether you will use conventional change journey stages from an *existing* model (you can research the linear and cyclical models above for examples) or *create your own* customized change journey stages. Both conventional and customized can be linear *or* cyclical.

   Some people use **conventional** stages because they are:

   - Perceived as credible
   - Quick to implement
   - Generally accepted

Some people create **customized** stages because they are:

- Unique and specific for each employee persona
- Personalized for your business and organizational culture
- Insight-driven based on your research

APPLICATION OF WHAT WE HAVE LEARNED: *Creating Employee Change Journey Stages*

We pick up our case study about Oliver and Ariel, who are creating a change management plan for the launch of a cloud-based software designed to personalize the customer experience.

Oliver and Ariel have an approved Change Journey Map framework and personas. Now, it's time to write the **stages**, to fill in that empty portion of the map. They know they need to write each stage from the persona perspective, so they reviewed employee research previously conducted for insights. They created stages starting **early** in the transformation through the technology launch and anticipated upgrades and optimizations to maintain the relationship and keep communication lines open.

Oliver knew from experience how heated and **emotional** discussions can be about change journey **stages**. Some people are adamant that it should be linear, because of their emotional need for the transformation to just be over, e.g., *"Please! Make it stop!"* Other people understand that particularly with new marketing technology, realistically, the change experience is more cyclical. And, when it's done right, with each next change cycle, people feel **fewer uncertainties** and progress through the change journey in **less time** and with **less pain.**

Oliver knew he had to **listen actively** to people, to hear their uncertainties, questions, and ideas before proceeding. After he did a **listening tour** with people who would be impacted by the change, he thought through how to facilitate conversations and ideations to write change journey stages, recognizing that each persona needed their own Change Journey Map.

One of the ways that Oliver helped people understand was to use analogies that people deal with in their everyday life. For example, a smartphone software update, we've all been there and dealt with it. He reminded people about phone software updates from years ago and all the disruption it caused to personal lives...such as, how long it took, the errors, how the upgrade changed settings without you knowing, or how the upgrade would hijack your phone in the middle of the day. When people were reminded of these stories and realized how the upgrades have improved over time (note, I did not say they are perfect...I said that they have improved), people started to laugh and get it. Despite people feeling the need for the transformation "to just be over," they understood the natural cyclical nature of the change experience.

While Oliver had everyone's attention, he shared best practices for writing change journey stages, such as writing from the **employee perspective**, engaging people **early** in their change experience, using **colloquial** and **emotional** language, and staying with people **after** the initial launch and not leaving them out in the cold. He reminded everyone that we must **place people at the heart** of the transformation.

He scheduled an **ideation** with seven representatives across disciplines to get the process started. Predicting the intensity of this discussion, he scheduled the session on a Friday morning, requested that people did not schedule any afternoon meetings, and promised to feed people breakfast and lunch. (Yes, free food works!) He requested that everyone prepare and review previous work, such as insights from the persona research, Employee Change Journey micro-moments, and the four agreed upon personas, as these insights would help inform writing change journey stages. He reminded everyone to **listen** to others, and be **open**, **curious**, and **respectful**. Basically, he asked everyone to arrive intellectually, emotionally, and physically prepared.

So one ideation session was ambitious! Let's just say there were a few more meetings. But the bottom line is that the team did ultimately write change journey stages for all four personas.

Let's take a look at an example of change journey stages, mindsets, and emotions for one persona, "Pioneer Pam."

Note that this is an abbreviated example for demonstration. This book has size and color limitations. When you create your Change Journey Map, I recommend:

- Using colors, icons, and other visuals to make the map engaging and bring the persona to life
- Including all elements of the map on one page (persona, stages, mindsets, emotions)

Check out change journey stages and mindsets for "Pioneer Pam" on the next page.

CHANGE JOURNEY STAGES & PERSONA MINDSETS

Pioneer Pam
Tech Lover
Early Adopter

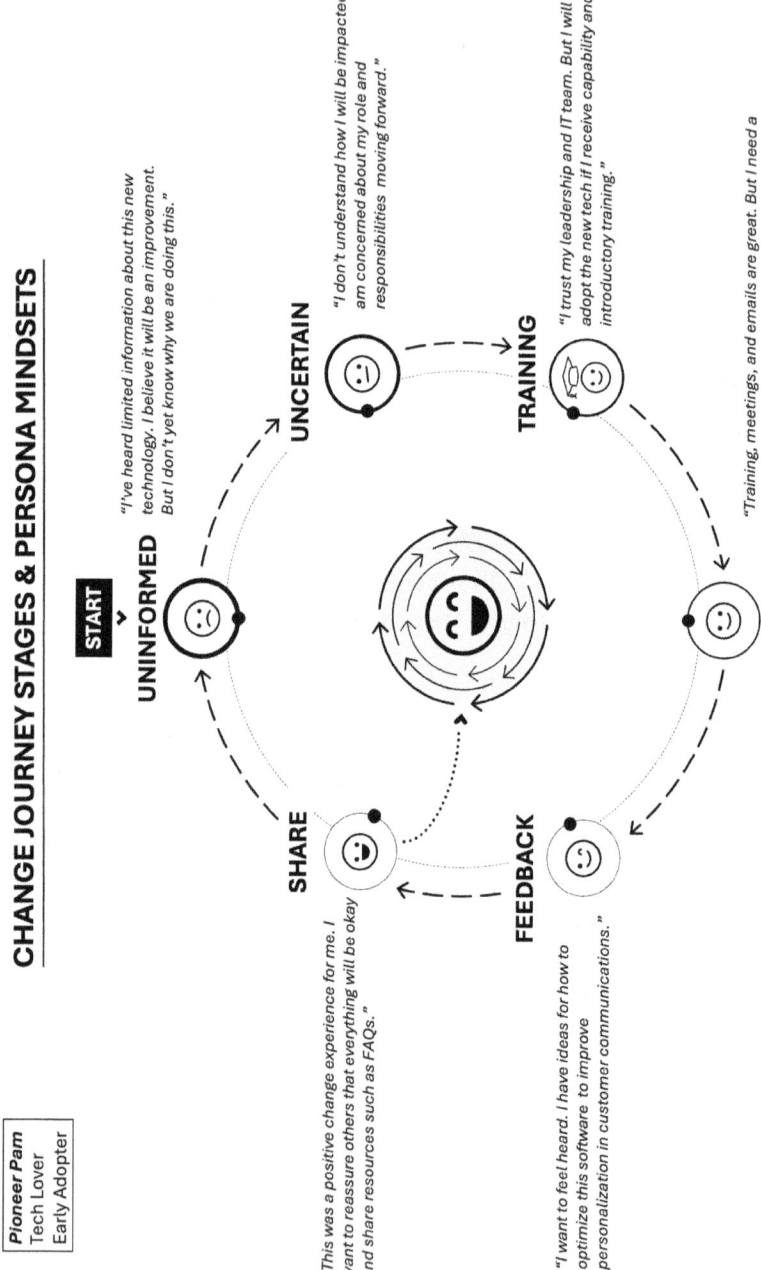

START

UNINFORMED

"I've heard limited information about this new technology. I believe it will be an improvement. But I don't yet know why we are doing this."

UNCERTAIN

"I don't understand how I will be impacted. I am concerned about my role and responsibilities moving forward."

TRAINING

"I trust my leadership and IT team. But I will only adopt the new tech if I receive capability and introductory training."

RESOURCES

"Training, meetings, and emails are great. But I need a central location where I can access all the information I need, when I need it, to feel confident."

FEEDBACK

"I want to feel heard. I have ideas for how to optimize this software to improve personalization in customer communications."

SHARE

"This was a positive change experience for me. I want to reassure others that everything will be okay and share resources such as FAQs."

INSIDER TIP

Linear, cyclical, or other? Conventional or customized? These can be **heated, emotional** conversations and decisions! Some people may feel adamant about their preference. Allocate **sufficient time** in your schedule for team discussions. A list of **pros and cons** can be helpful. Consider a **facilitator** to make sure everyone's point-of-view and rationale are heard, and assessments are inclusive and fair.

 KEY TAKEAWAYS

Let's summarize key takeaways about Employee Change Journey stages:

1. Employee change journey stages are t**he sequence of a persona's mindsets and behaviors during their change experience.**
2. Insightful change journey stages help **align** stakeholders and provide a **foundation** to choose relevant internal touch points and messaging.
3. Engage people **early** and **continue** the relationship through the transformation launch and sustainability.

Let's move on to chapter eight to complete the next section of our Change Journey Map, employee messaging.

*"Prove to people that you genuinely **care**."*

—Dina Shapiro

CHAPTER 8

CHANGE JOURNEY MESSAGING

Speak to the Heart and the Head

"I've learned that people will forget what you said, people will forget what you did, but people will never forget how you made them feel."
—Maya Angelou

 LEARNING OBJECTIVES

After reading this chapter, you will be able to define Employee Change Journey messaging, recognize its role and importance in the change journey, and write effective change journey messaging.

 CHANGE JOURNEY MESSAGING DEFINITION

Employee change journey messaging is:

What you communicate to employees throughout their change journey.

Let's break down that definition:

Communicate: To paraphrase from Cambridge Dictionary and Merriam-Webster Dictionary, the verb communicate is to share information with others by **speaking, writing, body language, or other signals.** This can be **one-way** or **two-way.** When people hear the word communicate, we often default to the speaking or writing part of the definition. I think it's important to remember that **body language** and other signals such as **tone** of voice contribute to what you communicate.

Employees: I'll say it again! Remember that critical word ~ *human* ~ in our definition of change management. We must place **people** at the **heart** of the change.

Throughout their change journey: We talked about the word "throughout" in Chapter 6 as important because it suggests an entire cycle versus a linear start and end. (I know, I know, people don't like hearing the word "cycle" because everybody just wants the transformation to end. But, in reality, this process typically is more cyclical than linear. However, with effective change management, rounds 2, 3, and so on of the cycle become less painful and much faster.)

THE BENEFITS AND ROLE OF CHANGE JOURNEY MESSAGING

Messaging is **one-way communication** that change leaders or managers share with the people who need to adapt to the change, or **two-way communication** between two or more parties, such as Q&A or feedback. Both are equally important.

Change messaging:

- **Informs people.** Although not everyone will agree with everything shared all the time, being informed is better than not being informed!
- Provides **information,** such as what this change is all about.
- Provides **access to information**, such as where to find a one-page summary of what was shared in a meeting.
- Provides **access to destinations,** such as a link to online training.

HOW TO WRITE CHANGE JOURNEY MESSAGING

Let's fill in the next section of our Employee Change Journey Map. Here are my ten steps to write Employee Change Journey messaging:

1. **How you say it counts.** People remember more about how you made them feel than what you said. What you say (your actual words) matters a lot, but if your "how" is off, then you'll *turn people off.*

2. **Balance rational and emotional messaging.** Rational messaging is important, such as describing the specifics of the transformation. It's also the easier part (note I did not say "easy," I said "easier" as a comparison to emotional). Because it's easier, we sometimes default to all rational messages. But we need to balance the rational with the emotional. The emotional messages connect and are more memorable. It's like that old saying, "It's not all *what* you say, it's *how* you say it." If you work in marketing

or advertising, you will eventually hear someone talk about "left brain" and "right brain". (Anyone laughing right now?) The Cleveland Clinic, a highly regarded global hospital system, discusses that the **left brain**, which is responsible for communication, problem solving, memorizing, and analyzing, and the **right brain**, which is responsible for creativity, intuition, emotional response, and imagination, **work together**. Change management must address **both** rational information and emotional benefits. For example, if your organization launches a new technology, *rational* information could include the technology capabilities and *emotional* reassurance could reiterate the employee's importance and role in the organization.

3. **Write Pragmatic, Simple, Painless (PSP) messaging.** Be **P**ragmatic. Don't try to shoot for the moon here. Stay grounded in the basics that people need to know. Keep it **S**imple. Avoid jargon or unnecessary information. Make it **P**ainless. Okay, so the transformation itself might have some pain, but *how* you communicate the *change story about* the transformation should be painless.

4. **Create messages that RISE.** Put all your messaging through this test: Does our message **RISE**? RISE = **R**eal, **I**nsightful, **S**traightforward, **E**mpathetic.

   Is it **R**eal? Are you being honest with people about the realities involved? Or are you sugar-coating? (That's bad, don't do that!)

   Is it **I**nsightful? Have you reviewed your research insights and personas to relate to people in a way that they will connect?

Is your message **S**traightforward? Or are you taking a windy road to share information? (That's bad, don't do that!)

Is your message **E**mpathetic? Are you thinking from the perspective of the people who will need to adopt this transformation every day?

You can even create a scorecard with a scale of 1 to 5 and rate your messaging to see if you meet the **RISE** goal.

5. **Consult with appropriate internal stakeholders**. Disciplines such as Internal Communications and HR can help you with the tone of the messaging. They can help with valuable insights about how, when, and where to share messaging. Keep them in the loop so they feel included and respected.

6. **Messaging must resolve uncertainties**. Remember in Chapter 2, I shared with you that the fear of change boils down to that one word: *Uncertainty*. Well, now is a great time to resolve those uncertainties!

7. **Create seamlessly integrated messaging**. Make sure your messaging aligns across the various internal touch points. It should vary to maximize the touch point capability. For example, a quick email can include reminders, and a link to a shared site with training can include more detailed information.

8. **Create the "change story."** This describes the change, why the change is happening, and the benefits of the change. The change story must clearly demonstrate

how the transformation objectives align with and help attain higher-level company vision or goals. (More about storytelling later when we discuss the Change Management Brief.)

9. **Share the right message from the right person.** The message can come **from** different sources, such as leadership, immediate supervisors, and peer-to-peer.

People tend to prefer high level or organization-wide messages from **leadership**, and more specific messages about changes, benefits, and implications for smaller teams and individuals from their **immediate supervisor.** According to Gallup, leadership plays a key role, but personalized internal communications make it easier for managers to build a bond with employees by resolving uncertainties and supporting the transformation.

Peer-to-peer is an opportunity for employees to communicate with each other. This can be a formal platform created for them, or casual discussion among themselves can be encouraged. Each person brings their knowledge and perspective to sharing information and problem-solving. Immediate supervisors and peer-to-peer tend to be more of a dialogue and two-way communication for questions and answers, problem-solving, and open conversation.

So high level organizational benefits are best communicated by leadership, whereas specific daily implications and individual benefits are best communicated by immediate supervisors.

10. **Create a feedback loop.** This hopefully will naturally occur in step #9 above. I recommend that you also create a formal process to collect feedback. This allows people to share their thoughts and concerns with those who have the power to help resolve those issues. Create a forum where people can ask questions and bring forth problems and challenges people have with the transformation. Share examples and case studies about how problems have been resolved.

APPLICATION OF WHAT WE HAVE LEARNED: *Writing Employee Change Journey Messaging*

We pick up our case study about Oliver, the CMO, and Ariel, the Marketing Director at an airline company, who are creating a change management plan for the launch of a cloud-based software designed to personalize the customer experience.

Enter: Deb, the Executive Creative Director of the company's internal agency.

Deb manages a large team of creative talent, including writers and graphic designers. She has experience writing internal employee communications, both at her current company and two previous companies. She and her team have strong writing skills that speak both externally to customers and internally with employees.

Deb knows the importance of collaborating with the HR and Corporate Communications teams, who are responsible for employee general and organization-wide communications. She has worked with them before on other projects to discover employee insights and lessons learned about what has worked well in the past or not, both for employees and leadership. She knows that they can also help with tone and language that may be sensitive or not well received within this organization's culture.

Ariel scheduled a kick-off meeting with Oliver and Deb to discuss the change management plan, the persona and change journey stages, mindsets, and emotions created so far. Deb's team was charged with writing messaging for each persona, for each journey stage, taking into account relevant persona insights, mindsets, uncertainties, and emotions.

Deb explained to the team the importance of balancing **emotional** messaging that speaks to the *heart* with **rational** information that speaks to the *head*.

She also discussed how her team would strive for **PSP** (**P**ragmatic, **S**imple, **P**ainless) and **RISE** (**R**eal, **I**nsightful, **S**traightforward, **E**mpathetic), when writing and evaluating their messaging ideas.

Deb reminded Oliver and Ariel about the *types* of messages that should come from *different* stakeholders. For example, high level transformation purpose and benefits would be best from leadership, whereas, tactical responsibility changes would be best from a direct supervisor.

Ariel mentioned that they would like to include a **feedback loop** to propel advocacy and sustain the transformation.

Let's take a look at an example of change messaging for one persona, "Pioneer Pam."

Note that this is an abbreviated example for demonstration. This book has size and color limitations. When you create your Change Journey Map, I recommend:

- Using colors, icons, and other visuals to make the map engaging and bring the persona to life.
- Including all elements of the map on one page (persona, stages, mindsets, emotions, messaging).

You can refer back to the previous chapter's visual to remind yourself about the mindset and emotion in each stage.

Check out change journey **messaging** for "Pioneer Pam" on the next page.

CHANGE JOURNEY MESSAGING

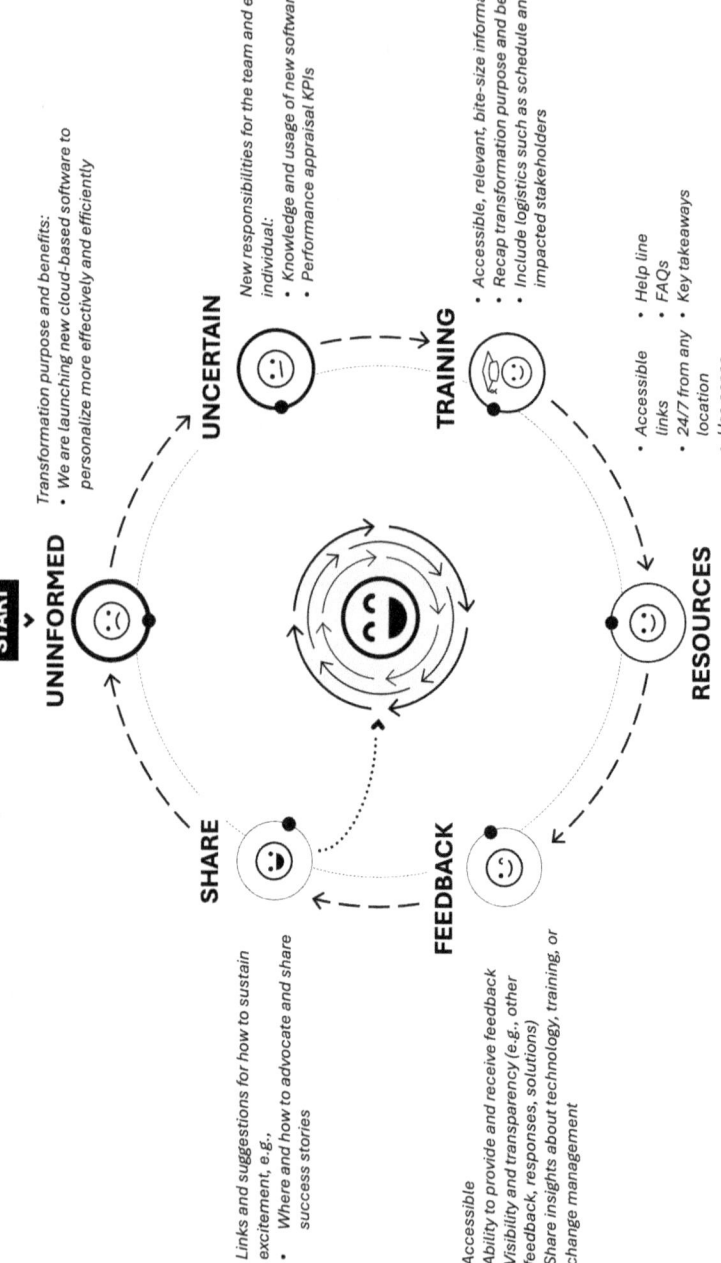

START

UNINFORMED

Transformation purpose and benefits:
• We are launching new cloud-based software to personalize more effectively and efficiently

UNCERTAIN

New responsibilities for the team and each individual:
• Knowledge and usage of new software
• Performance appraisal KPIs

TRAINING

• Accessible, relevant, bite-size information
• Recap transformation purpose and benefits
• Include logistics such as schedule and impacted stakeholders

• Accessible links
• 24/7 from any location
• Use cases

• Help line
• FAQs
• Key takeaways

RESOURCES

FEEDBACK

SHARE

Links and suggestions for how to sustain excitement, e.g.,
• Where and how to advocate and share success stories

• Accessible
• Ability to provide and receive feedback
• Visibility and transparency (e.g., other feedback, responses, solutions)
• Share insights about technology, training, or change management

Pioneer Pam
Tech Lover
Early Adopter

INSIDER TIP

Different people listen, remember, and learn in different ways, so you need to have a range of options for how you communicate, reinforce, and train people. A colleague of mine who has worked across senior positions in media, marketing, and brand strategy (yes, all three; he's a super talented and all-around terrific guy), whom I've known for a gazillion years, explains this brilliantly:

"You start with your first person, get them humming in their language, then take the best of that and then re-introduce it to the next person in a language they can understand. We assume there is one set of language for everybody, but that's where it falls apart, because different people have different languages. People digest information differently. The important thing is to understand that change means something different to everybody, and they will interpret what you tell them differently. Not everybody will sing the song the same way. It's like this group of people needs more strings, those people need more piano, and those over there need more of some other instrument."

I told you he was brilliant.

KEY TAKEAWAYS

Let's summarize key takeaways about Employee Change Journey messaging:

1. Employee change journey messaging is **what you communicate to employees throughout their change journey.**

2. Change journey messaging **informs** people with helpful information and provides **access** to information and destinations.
3. Balance **emotional** and **rational** insights throughout your messaging.

We are almost finished with our Change Journey Map! Our next chapter covers touch points, the final input to our map.

*"A touch point is any place your change story **comes into contact** with an employee."*

—Dina Shapiro

CHAPTER 9

CHANGE JOURNEY TOUCH POINTS

Communicate with Employees Where They Want

"Quality over quantity."
—Used by ancient philosophers to current influencers

 LEARNING OBJECTIVES

After reading this chapter, you will be able to define employee journey touch points, recognize their role and importance, and choose relevant touch points for employee change communications and experiences.

 CHANGE JOURNEY TOUCH POINTS DEFINITION

Employee change journey touch points are:

Where employees interact with internal change communications and experiences.

Let's break down that definition:

Where: This is the most important word in the definition! Touch points are the **places or environments** that change communications and experiences occur. They can be physical, virtual, or whatever.

Employees: I know, I know, I've said this already. But I'll say it again. We must place **people** at the **heart** of the change.

Interact: To paraphrase from Cambridge Dictionary and Oxford English Dictionary, an interaction is a direct **communication** or **reaction** between people.

Internal: A change management plan is an internal initiative for **employees only**. While most marketing transformations directly or indirectly affect customers or consumers, this book is focused on internal employees only.

Communications: We have **one-way** communication from leadership or change managers about the specifics of the change, including what, why, and benefits. We also have **two-way communication** such as real-time dialogue, feedback, or Q&A.

Experiences: As mentioned in the last chapter, this is when employees are affected through direct **observation** or **participation** in the transformation that affects how they feel.

Examples of internal touch points include Town Halls, weekly meetings, shared sites or intranets, email, newsletters, videos, ideations, staff meetings, and calls, just to name a few! But hang on, I'll share more examples in a minute.

BENEFITS AND THE ROLE OF CHANGE JOURNEY TOUCH POINTS

A touch point is a mechanism by which change managers can **reach** out to and **connect** with employees.

Finding **relevant** internal touch points helps change managers find opportunities to improve the Employee Change Journey.

Leveraging relevant touch points **positively** impacts how employees view the marketing transformation and their change experience.

Touch points **enable** employees to learn about transformation facts, timing, and benefits.

 HOW TO CHOOSE CHANGE JOURNEY TOUCH POINTS

So here's our last section to complete in our Employee Change Journey Map, my eight steps to choose change journey touch points:

1. **Use existing, regular firm-wide touch points.** Organizations from large to small have internal touch points you may use. There is no need to create new touch points for your change management plan. This will only raise questions, cause confusion, aggravate people ("*What? One more thing I need to learn*?!"), and possibly offend your colleagues who manage existing internal touch points ("*Huh? Why are you creating new touch points when we already have methods in place to communicate with employees?*"). Harness existing organizational mechanisms and norms.

2. **Use touch points throughout the persona's entire change journey.** Choose which touch points will be used for **each stage** of the change journey. Each stage should be populated with at least one touch point.

3. **Choose touch points that are relevant to your persona.** Customize how you reach people. Be where they are and where they prefer to engage with change communications and experiences.

4. **Choose the right touch points for each stage.** Review your persona and earlier research you conducted. Choose **quality** over quantity. Do not just include a touch point because it is available. Only choose touch points that are **relevant** to the **persona** and each of their change journey **stages**. When you prioritize quality over quantity, you can allocate your time, energy, and resources more effectively. Instead of spreading yourself thin by trying to be in every touch point, you can focus your efforts.

5. **Use a different mix of touch points in every change journey stage.** You can use *some* of the same touch points in various stages. You just don't want to have the *exact same mix* of touch points in *every stage* because it's harder for people to distinguish between different messages within those touch points. **Multiple** touch points help employees adopt the change as they progress through their change journey.

6. **Consider AI and other technological tools to help optimize your touch points mix.** These tools can help you choose the right mix of touch points at the right

stage and for the right message. They can also help you optimize the mix over time. AI can help personalize the choices based on preference data. AI can help augment your own internal research.

7. **Collaborate with your cross-discipline team.** Find which internal disciplines, such as HR or Internal Communications, and specific people who manage each of the internal touch points that you choose. Collaborate with your colleagues to incorporate the change story within those touch points in a mutually agreeable time and way.

8. **Assess the mix of touch points at your disposal.** There are multiple types of touch points to consider including:

   1. *Physical,* such as signage or posters at the company's location
   2. *Digital,* such as intranets, shared sites, or email
   3. *Print,* such as posters or brochures shared at a company event
   4. *Human,* such as weekly small team meetings, larger Town Halls, employee ambassadors, or video calls

Here's a **list of internal touch points** to consider, compliments of my amazing interviewees. Drum roll....it pretty much boils down to...**consider every touch point you have!**

Okay, you're about to read a **lengthy** list. I debated whether to streamline and edit this list of quotes but decided to keep it as-is because they are all just so great and helpful.

Get ready to hear **amazing ideas** from the **best of the best** marketers:

- *"Touch points will vary based on the size of your company. I work in a small company, so I communicate changes in a twice weekly call with the entire team for 1 hour. We go through everything. I don't use email because it can be misinterpreted, can feel like work, and it's hard to put emotion behind it or sell the change. But it could be a back-up but for a big change. I also use a division-wide call and sometimes Zoom for team calls."*

- *"All of them, anything, and go to lunch with people. No holds barred when choosing touch points."*

- *"Executive meetings. Team meetings. Surveys. Office hours or lunch and learns. Instead of people being talked at, make it more conversational. We do everything on Slack, so I guess you could use a Slack channel for feedback and questions."*

- *"I did a Town Hall for 700 people. The executive team was present. We created great training videos. Ask yourself what are the different ways that people get and absorb information and meet all of them. Get something out there for everybody. Keep hitting it home. Every new message, hit it multiple times in multiple places."*

- *"I use all of them! Contests, videos, guides, conference calls, All-Hands calls, Town Halls, face-to-face, go around the world and do lunch and learns and train people, go to local markets, train, 1:1 training and conversations, emails, and the intranet."*

- *"Use people managers as communication channels. Give them talking points, FAQs, training tools, and whatever else they need."*

- *"Do something important and personal."*

- *"Depends on the organization. At my last company, when we did their re-education and big branding workshops, we explained the brand segmentation to employees—brand architecture, segmentation, different target audiences, different products—and what this all meant to the engineers. It's not a one-and-done, like, okay we did the transformation and we're off! But we need to educate, re-visit, re-visit, and become a central theme to how the company makes the change."*

- *"I like agile, so I do daily stand-ups especially with remote teams, 8:30am every day. It can be 5 minutes, a quick check-in, to make sure we are constantly moving the ball down the field and aligned. Outside of the team that is managing and executing, I like a branded email that comes out at whatever frequency. I share congratulations and success stories and keep everyone informed."*

- *"Face-to-face, such as Town Halls, to get in front of people, have a conversation, and allow them to ask questions. So much is one-way. Even on an intranet with a comments section. This is different than asking a question and getting an answer immediately— create a safe place together like a Town Hall and discuss their questions and fears and allow them to get responses immediately. Then send an email, we are proliferated, but it's a good reminder like a summary, especially if it's from a leader. Video is always good; it's more interactive and entertains more. People are more likely to listen especially if it's short to align with their attention span. Intranets are useful for a repository of everything that's been done so like if a new employee joins* or someone forgets about a schedule or training, here's a place to go for everything. And anything you can do to engage, such as interactive or gaming or add a challenge, award prizes—anything you can do to drive engagement— so they are motivated to pay attention."

- "Top of the house, senior leadership, for example, monthly roundtables with C-suite to update. Global Town Halls, quarterly or other, and each leader within three weeks does their organizational messages from the global Town Hall, then a cascade from there. Use those formal mechanisms. Also use informal, like "ask me anything," talk about specific aspects of change, a quasi-audience-employee led conversation about the change so people feel heard and demonstrate that there is a consideration of their questions. Some clients call them clinics. Three to four Change Managers have a moderated conversation with the people in the weeds, and organizational newsletters. Incorporate these conversations in ongoing conversations. Change is constant. Something will always be changing. So get people over that fear. Be willing to make a mistake, think differently to get people in that comfort zone to navigate that change."

- "In the course of regular firm-wide existing mechanisms and piggyback off that, versus creating new ones. Town Hall. Regular management update. Part of sales meetings, for example, how is this transformation helping you do your job. Leverage existing cultural norms and mechanisms and do not create new ones. But use all the touch points at your disposal, keep hammering the messages, keep asking questions about problems and challenges people are having and fix them, and get success stories to share with others.

Share good case studies and examples of what works well, why, and how you can adapt or use something new."

- *"Must cascade down the organization quickly, and with all cascades, things get lost in translation. People more readily accept guidance from their direct supervisor vs. the top. Once you are a couple of levels removed, the top execs are not the ones with credibility, it's the direct supervisors who must be enrolled and early on. You need champions or ambassadors at lower ranks. Change becomes difficult because there's too much space between the proponent of the change like leaders, and those who are impacted everyday like mid or junior levels, so you need this representation."*

- *"For the cascade, differentiate between how to engage senior managers, people managers, functions, regions."*

- *"Use existing organization internal touch points; there is no need to create new touch points which will just require education and explanation."*

- *"Use them all and figure out what your organization reacts to. At my company, I would use Town Halls to draw attention to people who took the plunge and succeeded. I would use emails intermittently to say, 'Hey we just figured this out, or over the next few weeks we will be doing XYZ.' So, there is no set mode. Think about how people digest information. Figure out how do people consume information and meet them where they live. It may be somewhat intuitive but for others it isn't. But I can take more people on a journey when I connect with them."*

And there you have it, my friends.

APPLICATION OF WHAT WE HAVE LEARNED: *Choosing Employee Change Journey Touch Points*

We pick up our case study about Oliver, the CMO, Ariel, the Marketing Director, and Deb, the Creative Director at an airline company, who are creating a change management plan for the launch of a cloud-based software designed to personalize the customer experience.

Enter: Louis, the Chief Media and Experience Officer of the internal agency.

Louis has been with the company over 10 years, longer than Oliver, Ariel, and Deb. He has great knowledge of the company's history with internal communications, and particularly with his previous co-workers' change *mismanagement*. He has much value to add to choosing the right touch points at the right change journey stages for employees.

Louis reiterated the importance of using **existing touch points inside the organization** and to avoid creating new touch points that would cause confusion and unnecessarily increase costs and lengthen the schedule.

He suggested that the team use *different* touch points for *each persona* and a *mix* and range of touch points across each persona's change journey to maximize the message and experience.

He also reminded the team that supervisors and managers should meet 1:1 with individuals on their team to discuss role and responsibility changes, respond to questions real time, and collect feedback.

Louis said that certain touch points are more appropriate than others given the message and source. For example, broader messages for the entire team impacted by the change, or announcing and describing the transformation purpose and benefits should come from leadership in wider-reaching touch points, such as Town Halls.

He shared the importance of simple, quick access to resources, such as FAQs, training links, and feedback loops, which should be shared across as many touch points as possible to remind people of the availability.

Lastly, Louis suggested keeping it fun, such as contests and gamification in some of the touch points to keep people engaged.

Let's take a look at an example of change journey touch points for one persona, "Pioneer Pam."

Note that this is an abbreviated example for demonstration. This book has size and color limitations. When you create your Change Journey Map, I recommend:

- Using colors, icons, and other visuals to make the map engaging and bring the persona to life.
- Including all elements of the map on one page (persona, stages, mindsets, emotions, messaging, and touch points).

You can refer back to the two previous chapters' visuals to remind yourself about the persona mindset and emotions in each stage and messaging created by the change management team for each stage to mitigate uncertainties.

Check out change journey **touch points** for "Pioneer Pam" on the next page.

CHANGE JOURNEY TOUCH POINTS

Pioneer Pam
Tech Lover
Early Adopter

UNINFORMED
- Leadership emails and Town Halls
- Team emails from direct managers
- Discipline-specific meetings and emails

UNCERTAIN
- Small team meetings
- 1:1 conversations with managers

TRAINING
- Range of formats, e.g.,
  - Workshops
  - Synchronous and synchronous online
  - Mobile app

RESOURCES
- Office hours
- Online
- Phone
- Chat

FEEDBACK
- Online link
- Team meetings
- Town Halls
- Change ambassadors

SHARE
- Internal blog
- Team meetings

INSIDER TIP

It's hard to personalize touch points for personas. Personalizing internal touch points is easier by disciplines, individual teams, locations, or distribution lists created for smaller groups of people.

Realistically, there will be some employee self-selection through messaging in a touch point. For example, let's say you have three personas. You may have one email that is distributed to everyone in the marketing department with three different headlines or paragraphs, each with links to "If this is you, click here to learn more," which takes different people to different places with different content or experiences. There are lots of tactics for people to self-select messaging within a touch point, such as a quick three-to-five question survey they take, that leads them to relevant, personalized messaging for each persona.

Touch point decisions by persona tend to be easier (*not* easy, just *easier* compared to above) in live meetings, that are small or 1:1, in person or by video.

 KEY TAKEAWAYS

Let's summarize key takeaways about Employee Change Journey touch points:

1. Employee change journey touch points are **where** employees interact with internal change communications and experiences.

2. Touch points help change managers **interact** with employees as they progress through their change journey.
3. Use **existing** internal touch points to engage with employees **where** and **how** they prefer.

Congratulations! You have learned how to create an employee Change Journey Map. Next, we will discuss how to bring this map to life in a change story through a Change Management Brief.

*"**Inspiring** change journey stories start with an inspiring Change Management Brief."*

—Dina Shapiro

CHAPTER 10

THE CHANGE MANAGEMENT BRIEF

Create an Honest, Open, and Real Change Story

"A good insight can fuel a thousand ideas."
—Phil Dusenburry

 ## LEARNING OBJECTIVES

After reading this chapter, you will be able to define a Change Management Brief, describe its role and benefits, and create a Change Management Brief template.

 ## CHANGE MANAGEMENT BRIEF DEFINITION

An employee Change Management Brief:

Provides strategic guidance for the creation of the Employee Change Journey story, communications, and experiences.

Let's break down that definition:

Strategic: The detailed plan for what we would like the change communications to **achieve**. This is just like a Creative Brief that details what we want a customer creative campaign to achieve. The Change Management Brief needs to be strategic, **without dictating** creative specifics.

Guidance: This is **help** and **advice** for the team creating the change communications (which most definitely should include writers and graphic designers) as they consider different options for **how** to communicate. Note that I do not use the word "direction," which feels more like an order or instructions. This is kind of like, someone can offer advice about a few different routes to drive somewhere, or they can give you directions for one specific route to get there. When it comes to the creative process (which this is!), let's give the creative team the **flexibility** to **create**.

Employee change journey story, communications, and experiences: We've established that this change communications plan is for internal **employee** use only. (Yes, customers sometimes need change communications if the marketing transformation directly affects them, but that's external marketing and a different book.) The internal change story communications and experiences continue **throughout** the entire change journey cycle. Note the word "communications" is plural; the sum of each individual communication across multiple touch points throughout the entire change journey will be told as the **change story**.

THE ROLE AND BENEFITS OF A CHANGE MANAGEMENT BRIEF

Benefits of a properly written Change Management Brief include:

- **Aligns** stakeholders on **expectations** for change communications
- **Eliminates** confusion about the project scope and deliverables
- Ensures **consistency** between the change communications and **marketing transformation** purpose
- Provides detailed information and **insights** to **customize** change communications, including **mitigating uncertainties**
- Aligns the **personality** and **tone** of change communications with the organization's values or culture and brand personality
- **Saves you time** (and budget and headaches) because conflicts and disagreements are resolved earlier in the process ("measure twice, cut once")
- **Inspires** the team who will create the change communications

So basically, creating change communications **without a brief** is like trying to assemble furniture that arrives to your home in a bunch of pieces **without directions**. I mean I guess you can do it, but it's harder, takes more time, and you'll probably make unnecessary mistakes that force you to dismantle what you put together so far and go back to the first step. It's also frustrating and creates arguments if more than one person is involved. My head hurts even thinking about this!

However, creating change communications **with a brief** is like putting together the furniture **with** directions. And, even with directions, we can still make mistakes, feel confused, or have different interpretations or expectations.

So I recommend that you **review the brief with the people creating the communications** (writers, graphic designers) to make sure they're cool with it or discuss changes that should be made to the brief before they get to work.

(I know, I used the previously criticized word "direction" above, but this is just an analogy, so please go with it!)

Yup, you marketers guessed it. The benefits are **similar** between a Change Management Brief for internal employee change communications and a Creative Brief for customer or consumer campaigns. Remember that earlier chapter when we talked about how marketers are uniquely qualified to lead change management for marketing transformations? Consider this additional rationale.

HOW TO WRITE A CHANGE MANAGEMENT BRIEF

Each persona has its own Change Management Brief. When you complete each Change Management Brief template, answer each section specifically from the **perspective** of that **persona**.

Avoid generalizations that would be relevant to any persona. Speak in the language of the persona so they can relate.

Consult your **persona** insights and **Change Journey Map** for guidance about messages and experiences to include in your brief.

Consider formatting with a **maximum character count** in each section that will be completed. Remember, this is a Change Management *Brief*, so let's be as "brief" as possible with robust insights.

Design matters! Work with a graphic designer or art director to create an inviting template layout and style, using a nice font and visuals to differentiate between sections such as color coding or icons.

See the next page for Change Management Brief template thought starters.

CHANGE MANAGEMENT BRIEF TEMPLATE: THOUGHT STARTERS

1. Write **persona** highlights with a hyperlink to the full one-page persona summary.
2. **What** is the change?
3. What is the **one** change communications **objective**?
4. **Why** is this change happening?
5. What are the **benefits** of this change? Include emotional and rational.
6. **Why** should anyone believe that these benefits will really happen?
7. What change **uncertainties** are people feeling?
8. How will we **mitigate** the change uncertainties?
9. What is the **tone** of the change communications?
10. How would you describe the **change journey** in a maximum of five sentences? Include a hyperlink to the Change Journey Map that includes stages, touch points, and key messages.
11. What would we like people to **think, feel,** and **do**?
12. What are the anticipated **tensions, challenges,** and **difficulties**?
13. How will we **address** these anticipated tensions, challenges, and difficulties?
14. How can people provide **feedback** and review **responses**?
15. Where and how can people access **support** and participate in **training**?
16. How will the change communications be **measured** against the objective?
17. Summarize this **change story** in **one** sentence.
18. Include **links to insights** such as the entire Change Journey Map, examples of other well written completed Change Management Briefs, information such as timelines, and specific impacts that vary by disciplines.

The Change Management Brief can be used whether you create change communications internally, or with an external consultant or agency, or use a hybrid approach. Regardless of which one, you need to determine **who** will **write** the brief and participate in the **review-revisions-approval** process.

Yup, you saw the word **agency** in that last paragraph. Some foreshadowing here.... I'm a big fan of working with your agency partner to create the change story and communications. More about this later.

Here's a **list of best practices and ideas for the Change Management Brief to consider**—again—compliments of my amazing interviewees. You're about to read a **lengthy list**—again—which I kept as-is because these quotes are all just so great and helpful:

- *"You must communicate the benefit of the transformation but be realistic about the challenges. Everything has a price. So if a business decides to execute this transformation, they need to quantify the cost of not doing it vs. the cost of doing it, so it's a business decision, it will cost money, hurt, and be painful. But we will be better off on the other side of this."*

- *"The change story must communicate what, how, why, and benefits to the organization, team, and individual. What's in it for me? Why do I need to do something differently? Address the tendency people have, which is to focus more on limitations vs. the advantages they will receive. They are keenly aware of all the added hassle but pay less attention to what they will receive in return."*

- *"Link the reason for the change to the higher-level organizational vision, mission, or purpose to demonstrate alignment with higher level goals and objectives so people can embrace the change themselves and inspire others."*

- *"Need to get people excited about the change, and how it will help them, tie back to business or senior objectives at high level."*

- *"Help people understand why we need to shift the way we work or the way we do something."*

- *"Help people inside the process understand, okay, go through this, it will be annoying, but you will get to this better end state."*

- *"People who will just not get onboard with the change story, you need to act immediately, like rotate to another position within the company or exit them. It is better for everyone including those individuals."*

- *"Communications need to include access or links to assets, different versions for everything based on personas, regions, languages, or markets, and FAQs, timelines, training tools and templates."*

- *"Yeah, the obvious stuff...what's the change, why are we making the change, how will it benefit from as high up as possible in the organization—to the team—to each individual. By the way, this is why we need personas to hit the differences."*

- *"What will you no longer be doing to make time for new things you need to do, why, will someone else be doing it or will it no longer be done?"*

- *"What will suck in the short or immediate time frame, in the beginning of the transformation for the first couple of weeks? If we don't know, then remind people that we know something sucky will happen, but we don't yet know the specifics, and here's the place to tell us about what sucks so we can help you."*

- *"What do you need to Let Go Of?"*

- *"Be upfront and transparent and real that this is hard. It's hard to get people to rally around it."*

- *"Balance promise + reality."*

- *"Take the time to get your language and attitude together."*

- *"Delivery is important. Be authentic and believable and get the inertia out of the way."*

- *"People are always more comfortable with what they were doing yesterday. It's known, it's probably safe. Majority of people, you must pull along. Harness the ones who have equal amounts of vision, perspective, pride, and get-it-done attitude. It takes a few people to click. The click thing is important. The resistant people need to see that there is magic; otherwise, they can't believe."*

- *"Communicate the changes at both larger organizational, smaller team, and individual levels. What will happen, how will it happen, what is replacing people if there are layoffs? Be transparent about what and why."*

- *"Why is this better? Help people understand why and how it will impact their life with sensitivity to recognize that this will not feel better to most people until it becomes a habit or ritual as much as the last thing was. You must acknowledge what will stink at first.... yeah, you'll probably feel frustrated for a couple of weeks until you get the hang of it. We know we are asking you to do something that may feel frustrating."*

- *"Understand the human and emotional impacts of the change."*

- *"Acknowledge the realities. People need to be understood, so be empathetic, like yes, you will be frustrated for the first couple of weeks due to XYZ, so people will understand that, yes, I get that this will suck for the first two weeks, but I see that they know they are asking me to do something frustrating for a while."*

- *"Persuade people to embrace and inspire others."*

- *"Anticipate the pain, need key objection handling, understand the pain we are about to create and have answers for that pain, like a project bonus, a stay bonus for workforce reduction, etc."*

- *"Transparency about realities. Not every part of this will be good; just tell people the truth."*

- *"Overcommunicate, why, benefits, vision."*

- *"Deal with the reality. People claim that everyone is hungry for learning and wants to learn more, but this is such b*#^^s*$t. People do not have enough time. They have little interest in learning, even though it is in their self-interest. We need to help people overcome the balance between their day job and their feeling 'now you want me to learn something completely new?' even though in everyone's hearts, they know that it's good."*

- *"Need the global narrative."*

- *"We have communications every day for a project we're doing, and still there are people who have no idea what we are doing despite all the contests, videos, guides, conference calls, all-hands calls, everything we can do to deliver the message. Our strategy has been to go for fun, not just bullet points. We have Dad's joke of the week, like some stupid joke, like what does the janitor say when he jumps out of the closet—SURPRISE! Needs to be fun. We do newsletters on Fridays, that's fun and make them smile and laugh."*

- *"FAQs."*

- *"Head + Heart. You need to share the rationale stuff but connect emotionally with people or you'll never get the transformation off the ground."*

- *"Get people Change Journey Ready."*

And there you have it, my friends.

APPLICATION OF WHAT WE HAVE LEARNED: *Creating a Change Management Brief Template*

We return to Ariel, Oliver, Deb, and Louis to conclude their case study with how they wrote their Change Management Brief template.

Let's take a step back and review some context.

The team was excited to have their completed, approved personas and Change Journey Maps, including stages, mindsets, emotions, messaging, and touch points.

Remember, this cross-discipline team has a mix of change management experience, seniority, and tenure at the organization. Let's recap who's on our team:

> **Ariel,** the **Marketing Director**, is learning change management during this project by applying her marketing skills, experience, and traits to marketing transformation change management. Her confidence is growing at each step in the process.
>
> **Oliver,** the **CMO**, has excellent change management capabilities from his experience at previous companies, albeit not at this current company. While he is confident in his change management abilities, Oliver understands the importance of collaborating with others who have more insight about how things work at this company.
>
> **Deb**, the internal agency's **Executive Creative Director**, has experience writing internal employee communications, both at her current company and

two previous companies. She has much value to add from all of her experiences.

Louis, the internal agency's **Chief Media and Experience Officer**, has been at the company the longest. Over the years, he has led many internal communications initiatives, including choosing optimal touch points for different messages and experiences. He recognizes the value he brings and is open to other points of view and ideas to keep the approach fresh and current.

Given this team's collective experience in creative and campaign development, they are certain of the **role** and **importance** of a Change Management Brief as a springboard for the creative team of writers, art directors, and graphic designers to create **relevant, engaging, personalized change journey communications and experiences**.

However, there was no Change Management Brief **template**.

So the team got to work creating a template. They applied their skills, experience, and knowledge about Creative Brief template best practices for customer campaigns.

See the next page for a few *highlights* of items the team included in their marketing transformation **Change Management Brief template** along with their tips for how to complete each section.

CHANGE MANAGEMENT BRIEF TEMPLATE

- **Persona:** Which persona is this brief for? Include a few highlights here, with a link to the full persona summary for deeper insights. Remember, whatever you write here will guide how you complete the rest of this template.
- **Describe the marketing transformation:** In one sentence, what is changing? Speak in a language that everyone will understand. In one more sentence, what is leadership's vision for making this change? This is the *why* that applies across all impacted stakeholders.
- **What uncertainties need to be mitigated?** List up to three bullet points of this persona's uncertainties that must be resolved in order for them to adopt the marketing transformation.
- **What is benefit of this change?** In one sentence, from the persona's perspective, answer, "W*hat's in it for me?*" This is a good place to connect emotionally with people. There likely will be additional or tactical benefits, which can be communicated through training and 1:1 conversations with managers. Focus here on the single, most important benefit.
- **What are the support points for the benefit?** What rational reasons to believe or proof points can you share? In a maximum of three bullet points, answer from the persona's perspective, "W*hy should I believe the benefit?*"
- **What would we like the persona to think-feel-do?** For your persona, describe in one sentence each, what you would like them to *think* differently, *feel* differently, and *do* differently.
- **Share the anticipated pain points.** Be honest and forthright about what you expect to be difficult for people.
- **Measurement.** Agree to how the change management will be measured. Be careful here to focus on change management KPIs, not KPIs only specific to the marketing transformation. The latter is not completely in your control.

The team requested feedback from a few impacted stakeholders, including the internal creative team. After several productive, respectful conversations, they incorporated the feedback and finalized the template. Deb's team took the template information and created an inviting, user-friendly design with engaging, differentiating visuals and color coding.

From this point, the team worked on writing the Change Management Brief, aka, *filling in the blank spaces on the template*. Remember that creating your template is step 1 and super important. Even harder is step 2, *filling in those blank spaces* on the template. Leave yourself plenty of time to think, write, edit, and request feedback from the team, especially the creative team who will be creating the internal campaign.

After the recommended Change Management Brief was shared with the three creative teams working on this initiative, Ariel met with each person individually. They wanted to understand what, if any, impact the new Change Management Brief template had on the process. The creative teams agreed to complete three anonymous surveys, pre-during-post change story creative campaign development.

Ariel decided to augment the creative team's survey feedback with additional impacted stakeholders for a larger research sample size.

After the change management campaign launched, Ariel reviewed all the surveys from impacted stakeholders. The feedback was stellar. In pre-during-post surveys, respondents were asked to rank a series of criteria by:

1. Completely agree
2. Somewhat agree
3. Neither agree nor disagree
4. Somewhat disagree
5. Completely disagree

The survey results revealed that 97% of respondents completely agreed that the change management campaign *"resolved my uncertainties,"* and 92% completely agreed that it *"spoke to me personally."*

And...that's a wrap for the Ariel-Oliver-Deb-Louis case study!

 INSIDER TIP

Write a Change Management brief to inspire your **change story**. Think about key **elements** in a good **story,** such as the lesson, conflict, characters, plot, resolution (aka, resolving **uncertainties!**), dialogue, emotion, and hooks. Bring this transformation to life by **connecting** with people through **storytelling**. How will your change **story evolve**? How will people **participate** in the change story? How will you **customize** the story for different personas? How will you acknowledge expected **challenges** and **pain**?

Decide when or where in the change journey to use **integrated** and/or **transmedia** touch points to tell your change story. *Integrated* is the same message across touch points.

Transmedia is different messages in different touch points to reveal different information, create different experiences, or entice people to engage in different touch points.

 ANOTHER INSIDER TIP

When writing the change story from the Change Management Brief, look at the problem by **inversion**, aka, **solve a hard communication problem by thinking of it backwards**.

Sure, you can brainstorm all the ways to persuade people to adopt a marketing transformation; that's expected. But if you **also** look at the challenge by **inversion**, you will think about what to communicate to *discourage* (yes, I said *discourage*) people from adopting the transformation.

This is a great **exercise** to **uncover uncertainties employees believe and associate with the marketing transformation,** which can lead to super **creative thinking, copy, and training**.

This thinking is inspired by Charlie Munger, billionaire business partner of billionaire Warren Buffett. He is quoted as saying, *"All I want to know is where I'm going to die, so I'll never go there."* His thinking was inspired by the German mathematician Carl Gustav Jacob Jacobi, who solved some difficult problems by following this strategy: *"man muss immer umkehren"* (or loosely translated, *"invert, always invert"*). Meaning, per Munger, that, *"many hard problems are best solved when they are addressed backward."*

Source consulted: *"Inversion and The Power of Avoiding Stupidity,"* fs (Farnam Street Media Inc.), Shane Parrish, Former Canadian Spy and guru of lots of things. Check out references in the back of this book for links to read more about this source and sign up for fs newsletters. Quite interesting stuff, really.

 KEY TAKEAWAYS

Let's summarize key take ways about the Change Management Brief:

1. A Change Management Brief provides **strategic guidance** to create internal change journey communications.
2. A Change Management Brief **aligns** stakeholders, **mitigates or eliminates uncertainties,** and **inspires** people.
3. You need **creative professionals,** such as creative directors, writers, or graphic designers, to provide **feedback** and be **comfortable with and excited about** the brief **before** initiating creative development

That wraps up the strategic part of this book. Next up is implementation—process and stakeholders—for which I have new ideas, tips, and approaches for you. Let's read on.

*"The power of process is seriously **underestimated.**"*

—Dina Shapiro

CHAPTER 11

THE CHANGE MANAGEMENT PROCESS

Place People at the Heart of the Marketing Transformation

"The secret of getting ahead is getting started. The secret of getting started is breaking your complex overwhelming tasks into small manageable tasks and starting on the first one."
—Mark Twain

 LEARNING OBJECTIVES

After reading this chapter, you will be able to define key steps in a change management process that places people at the heart of the marketing transformation.

CHANGE COMMUNICATIONS PROCESS FOR MARKETING TRANSFORMATIONS

A change management plan and strategy are only as good as the **implementation**. I know you know this because it's just like in marketing. You can have a great marketing plan and strategy, but if the implementation is bad, well, you have a problem on your hands.

A best practice **process** is the difference between **success** and **failure** of each and every employee's change journey.

A process that places *people at the heart* of the transformation requires two categories: **human** and **procedural**. Let's dive into the "how to" for each one.

HUMAN

Collaborate with internal *and* external stakeholders. More about this in the next chapter, but the headline here is to bring in the right **people**, at the right time, in the right way, for the right reasons.

Make training available, accessible, and engaging. Different **people** need different training experiences, including a variety of content, formats, lengths, and frequency. Be creative, use training design best practices, and create interactivity. Start training as soon as possible and follow through to ensure employee uncertainties are resolved and people feel **psychologically safe.** Consider **training pilots** with just a few **people** to get feedback and make improvements, prior to the full roll-out. Is it robust enough? What's missing? What's good? Do we have the correct formats? How are our tools and templates? Do we have the right post-training support?

Relevant, accessible, engaging training is a major opportunity! Think this is obvious? Or not sure if you believe me? Well, then listen to what *HR Today* published:

- **44%** of employees do **not** agree that their company provides adequate training opportunities
- **74%** of dissatisfied employees prefer to work for an employer that provides **easy access** to training
- **60%** of employees prefer to access training through a mobile device, but only 19% have access to this option

Determine how you will share information with the cross-discipline change management team. Consider a range of touch points such as a shared site, emails, and live meetings to make sure you accommodate all **people's** needs and preferences.

Continuously refer to your transformation purpose and employee personas. Keep internalizing the direction and insights throughout the change management process to keep **people** at the heart of the change and maintain project focus.

Create a feedback loop. This starts at the beginning of the process and continues throughout. Create a safe environment so **people** feel *comfortable* speaking up and honestly. Be *forthright* about timing, steps to address feedback, and how feedback will be resolved. **Feedback** is a critical component of a change management program, so allow me to dive in a little more deeply here:

- **Make it easy for people to share feedback and make sure to act on that feedback.** According to Deloitte, a global management consultancy, 90% of workers say they are more likely to stay with an employer that accepts and acts on feedback.

- **Be direct, transparent, and realistic with people when and how you respond to feedback.** Here's an analogy to support my point. Per National Geographic, changes in matter can be either physical or chemical. **Physical** changes are **reversible**, like when an ice cube melts to water and then can freeze again. **Chemical** changes are **not reversible**, like when a log burns to ashes, you cannot then change those ashes back to a log.

  How does this relate to feedback? Well, a solution to complaint "A" could be like a **physical** matter change. You **can** reverse, modify, or correct it, such as communicating more or less frequently or in different touch points, or involving managers more or less. Whereas a solution to complaint "B" may be like a **chemical** matter change. You **cannot** reverse or modify it, such as an idea that does not align with the transformation purpose or excludes relevant stakeholders.

- **Respond to all feedback.** Most people do *not expect* that *all* their suggestions will be implemented. However, **people want to feel heard.** Share how suggestions or issues are being addressed. It's okay to tell people that you are not moving forward with a suggestion so long as you explain why and align your response with the transformation purpose or some other objective element of the change management plan or transformation scope.

Share success stories! Share good news! Share gratitude when people do things well! Share these things loudly and frequently. Don't wait for a quarterly meeting or when someone asks a question. As William Arthur said, *"Feeling gratitude and not expressing it is like wrapping a present and not giving it."*

Positives can be anything, such as:

- We're ahead of schedule by six days!
- We're still on budget!
- Training has 96% attendance!
- We've seen lots of transformation advocacy in our internal employee blog!
- 88% of people say they're more satisfied with their everyday work after they became comfortable with the transformation!

PROCEDURAL

Before I share some new ideas, let's briefly recap procedures from previous chapters:

Gather insights from employee research. Start with an audit of available insights internally and externally. HR is a good place to start for this information. Augment with external searches and custom research specifically for marketing transformation change management.

Create employee personas. This is not one actual person. This is a good ol' exercise in segmentation, just like you do for external customers. Create three to four employee personas specific to marketing transformations. Review available employee research. Augment with custom internal research to discover insights to place employees at the heart of the transformation.

Build your Employee Change Journey Map. Dive into each persona to think from the employee's perspective. Each persona has its own Change Journey Map. Think through the change journey stages and decision criteria to help people progress from one stage to the next. Determine customized messaging and relevant internal touch points for each stage.

Write your Change Management Brief. This focuses on the change story aspect of the change journey experience. Include valuable details and insights so the writers and graphic designers can create relevant communications that engage and inspire everyone involved in the transformation.

Here are even more procedural ideas to augment what I shared in previous chapters:

Design a one-page summary of your change management plan. Make it clear, readable, and inspiring. Use this for check-ins with leadership, executive sponsors, and as a reference tool during team meetings. It reminds everyone about what you're doing, why you're doing it, and keeps people aligned. Include information such as transformation purpose, change management steps or activities, success criteria, stakeholders, and key dates.

Create templates for everything possible! Templates facilitate team alignment and save time throughout the process. Templates can be created for the process, responsibility charting (more about this in the next chapter), schedules, feedback, personas, Change Journey Maps, Change Management Briefs, measurement, results, optimization plans, and lessons learned for the next transformation. Use software available within your organization or consider obtaining tools to work efficiently.

Create a schedule. Marketers are well versed in how to create schedules and the benefits of sharing schedules, keeping schedules current, and keeping **on time**. My client who has run L&D at three global agencies tells me all the time:

"Mind the timing and schedule. When it takes longer, it creates frustration if you're the one driving the change or transformation, and anyone who's a naysayer will then say that this f*#!*ng transformation isn't working."

Create a central repository of all information, training, FAQs, feedback loops, whom to contact, you know, basically everything. This is necessary for when people change roles, leave the organization, or when new people join the team (i.e., knowledge transfer). People love **use cases,** so keep uploading and providing them along with lessons learned. A use case is an example of how you used or applied the transformation. Theory is great, but practice is even better.

Measure and optimize. According to Prosci, 63% measure compliance with the change and overall performance to meet project objectives. (Jeez, you'd think this number would be 100%. I mean, really. Nobody would approve or fund a marketing campaign without measurement!!) But here's an even more interesting insight from their study: Of those who do measure, **76% meet or exceed change project objectives,** compared to only 24% who do not measure and meet or exceed project objectives.

DINA L. SHAPIRO

So basically, when you measure (like what 63% of people do), you seriously up your chances to meet or exceed your change management marketing transformation objectives!

If you're in the 37% of people who do not measure, you're probably facing some barriers, including disagreement about objectives, how to attain those objectives, or how to assess whether or why those objectives have been achieved.

Whether you fall into the 63% or 37% of those who do or do not measure, let me bring something important to your attention. Per BCG, a global management consultancy, here are some challenges to **measure** the **training** aspect of your change management program (so this relates to everyone, whether you currently do or do not measure your impact):

- **It's hard to determine the metrics.** Yes, you can track the time an employee spends on training. But tracking the *application* of that training and learning through someone's everyday workflow is different.

- **It's hard to isolate the variables to distinguish correlation from causation.** Let's say an employee's performance has improved since the training. Has their performance improved due to the training (causation) or is it simply a correlation (or what some may call a coincidence)? How do you know whether it's due to *training* or *another factor*? Maybe they had help from their manager or colleague. Maybe they were motivated by uncertainty about their job status or whether they will continue to be assigned to high visibility projects.

- **The impact of a training session or program usually is not immediately apparent.** It takes *time* to acquire

CHANGE MANAGEMENT FOR MARKETERS

skills and apply them to everyday work demonstrated by business impact.

- **Different leaders or managers may have different expectations and motivations for training.** That means, there may be *no agreed upon* measure of success. Some may look for productivity improvements, others may look for improved retention, and others may look to improve their brand's recognition or relevance.

Depending on your organization's resources and commitment to change management initiatives, your ability to solve the above items will vary. At the minimum, be aware of these issues, discuss them with your team, and do your best.

Bottom line, **people need to talk with each other.** It's the best way to find out how everyone is responding to the transformation in terms of their feelings and behaviors. If you ask, people will tell you. You just have to give them the opportunity to be heard and feel safe to speak honestly.

Here's a list of **best practices and ideas** to consider for **measurement** and **metrics**—again—compliments of my amazing interviewees. Yup, this list is **lengthy** too. But it has lots of juicy ideas for you to use.

- *"Important, you must share results broadly. You can fall in love with your own results. But someone from another team might be able to identify something that you don't see. For example, you have good results, but you hear from another discipline like the call center that they have complaints. It gets people excited when they feel involved and contribute, so they buy in more and add ideas."*

- *"Keep testing new things, get feedback, make changes and be obvious about it. Like, we heard such and such feedback, made such and such change, so let us know how this goes, and keep the feedback coming."*

- *"Set objectives and ensure the entire organization knows the purpose of the change, their role in changing, and what the outcome will be for them and the benefit to them. 'What does this mean for me?' is the first question everyone has. Focus on the individual as much as the enterprise."*

- *"You need to benchmark, you need that baseline, the starting point for comparison."*

- *"The team needs to create a dashboard, maybe a one-page quick read that anyone can access at any time. Post it where anybody can read it."*

- *"I'm the technology CRM guy, so I focus on that type of stuff. You need to manage the central repository of source of truth. Need to manage this information, clean it, and make sure the data is accurate; otherwise, it all falls apart. Requires sales and marketing to join hands and work together to ensure seamless hand-offs and continue to manage what happens to that customer over time to get the right data. The CRM must be set up correctly and connect to the right other systems to accurately give you the measurement and ROI."*

- *"Measure the qualitative, for example, enthusiasm, ideas, the human side of the change."*

- *"Does the internal marketing transformation have external benefits, such as sales or market share growth, and internal benefits like saving time or reducing costs."*

- *"Do a survey, create your own, or add questions to a current or ongoing employee engagement survey."*

- *"What behavior are we trying to change, and has it changed?"*

- *"Adoption of the transformation itself."*

- *"How many clicks or hits to newsletters with the change story, or how many people view the information that we provide?"*

- *"How many people show up, attendance, to conference calls, town halls, meetings, and such?"*

- *"How many people took the training?"*

- *"How many people downloaded the information?"*

- *"Is the message, the whole change story, getting through to people?"*

- *"Vision + People + Resources. Need to get this aligned and to click. All levers need to be flipped at the same time. Pull the band-aid off quickly. Do not pretend. Be clear and upfront about what we are doing and how we will do it. Do not carry naysayers or those who refuse to adapt too long. Make decisive changes and move forward. Part of measurement and optimization is dealing with really hard s*!t like firing people who just aren't on the train. If they're under the train, get them off the tracks before the train rides right over them; you're actually doing them a favor."*

- *"Pre- and post-surveys of training, communications, are they still understanding and using or doing the change?"*

- *"Operations, how much of the new process or system that was implemented is being used, such as a new CRM?"*

- *"Poll people, ask whether the marketing transformation is helping them in their daily job, why or why not, how does it make your job better, are you clear how to use it, do they get the vision of the marketing transformation?"*

- *"Do you feel more or less uncertain about the marketing transformation, your role in it, benefits to you?"*

- *"Excitement pre vs. post."*

- *"Employee confidence that they can do their job differently or better."*

- *"Clarity of communications."*

- *"Commitment of senior leadership."*

- *"Was information about the marketing transformation relevant or not? Why?"*

- *"Build questions into formal ongoing employee engagement survey."*

- *"Measure downloads of materials like FAQs or training key takeaways."*

- *"NPS of the transformation."*

- *"Satisfaction of this process, the whole thing.*

- *"Scale of 1 to 10, how well did this process go, then why, the verbatims."*

- *"Measure the marketing transformation itself, for example, better content, less time, etc."*

- *"How people feel about the change.*

- *"Measure adopt and sustain is to measure the marketing transformation effectiveness and usage itself."*

- *"Town Halls – switch from 100% lecture or presentation to fireside chats...look at the types of questions and pre- vs. post-event scores, are people more or less positive after the marketing transformation and change management?"*

And there you have it, my friends.

⌐ STEPS TO MEASURE AND OPTIMIZE CHANGE MANAGEMENT

Here are four foundational components to include in a change management measurement and optimization plan:

1. **Define success of the marketing transformation.**

   Remember, the transformation objectives may have been created way above your head, for example, upselling or cross-selling new customers through personalization, improving sales, reducing resources required to create marketing campaigns, etc. You may not have written these objectives. Yet the success of the marketing transformation will ultimately boil down to its adoption and sustainability.

   Although this is not 100% in your control and is not a specific change management measurement, *this information is required* to build out points #2-4 below.

2. **Determine change management accountability metrics by measuring its progress.**

Specific metrics *vary* by the type of transformation and change management program. For example:

- *Change management* performance, such as, "Have we effectively communicated the change and its benefits?"

- *Organizational*, such as, "Is the transformation delivering its purpose of more effective personalization with less money and decreased time of staff?"

- *Individual*, such as, how quickly the transformation was adopted, or if people feel better off after adopting the transformation.

3. **Assess whether the targeted impact has been achieved and why or why not.**

   Create a *dashboard*. Include each objective, the metrics for each objective, the benchmark or starting place, results, qualitative assessment to answer the "why" behind the results (some theory is okay but you need to talk with people 1:1 or through focus groups, surveys, town halls, etc.), and a comments section for how you will maintain the positives and address the negatives.

4. **Determine how to optimize change management to drive sustainability.**

   According to Prosci, projects with excellent change management are up to **7x** more likely to meet or exceed project objectives compared to those with poor or no change management. Of those who include sustainment in change management, **81%** meet or exceed objectives, whereas only 15% who did not include sustainment achieve the same results.

So to ensure the transformation's sustainability, keep *measuring* and *optimizing*, and implement train-the-trainer sessions to *continue the momentum* among those making the everyday changes.

 ## APPLICATION OF WHAT WE HAVE LEARNED: *Establishing a Change Management Process*

This is a case study about Lorraine, a Senior Project Manager working in a bank's credit card division, who established the organization's first *change management* process for marketing transformations.

Lorraine joined the bank five years ago as a Project Manager. Two years later, she was promoted to Senior Project Manager. Leadership promoted her due to her proactivity in establishing new processes in areas of the organization that lacked established, consistent, or best practice processes.

One day, Lorraine was having lunch with her colleague.

Enter: Bryan, a Customer Experience Manager.

Bryan joined the bank as a Customer Experience (CX) Manager for the largest product within the credit cards line of business (LOB). When he joined the bank, each credit card product had its own CX Manager. Leadership decided to centralize the CX discipline into one Center of Excellence (COE) across the entire credit card LOB.

Bryan was promoted to CX Director, charged with establishing the new CX COE and all its new processes. This charge had *a lot of legs.* Bryan's team needed to discover and eliminate customer pain points (also called irritants or dissatisfiers) across credit card journeys for both new and current customers. The current systems and data were manual and siloed. With no automation, people would need to listen to *thousands* of calls to get to the root causes of customer pain points, capture themes, and act on those insights to improve the CX. That could be optimizing marketing campaign messaging, the mobile app and website experiences, and creating ongoing training for customer service reps who take customer complaint calls. These are *just a few* examples. This would not be a "one-and-done" change, but rather an **ongoing systemic behavioral and cultural transformation.**

Is your head spinning?

Does this sound complex?

Yes, this is **one seriously complex marketing process transformation!**

Let's go back to Lorraine's lunch with Bryan. As he explained what he needed to accomplish, Lorraine told Bryan that he **needed change management to succeed.** She shared that awful statistic, that about *70% of transformations fail.* She explained the purpose and benefits of change management for marketing transformations, shared her experience in this area, and gave preliminary ideas right off the top of her head. Lorraine assured Bryan that with *effective change management, his transformation would succeed.*

Bryan was sold. He understood that he needed a **change process to manage his process changes**. He asked Lorraine to join his team to lead Project Management. Lorraine loves solving challenges and simplifying complexities, so she jumped on the opportunity.

Let's fast forward to **change management process highlights** that Lorraine established for Bryan's marketing transformation.

Lorraine is a big believer in *placing people at the heart of the transformation*, so she started with the **human and emotional** elements, and then moved on to **procedures** and **rational** information.

She outlined preliminary action steps such as:

- **Change Communications.** Review employee research to create personas, Change Journey Maps, and Change Management Briefs to create insightful, engaging change stories and experiences.
- **Training.** Create content including the transformation purpose, benefits, schedule, and new capabilities required. Determine training formats, frequency, and accessibility. Design personalized learning paths by personas.
- **Feedback.** Determine how to obtain and respond to feedback in a transparent, efficient, and effective way.
- **Success.** Create a method and communications plan to share success stories, use cases, and lessons learned.

- **Executive Summaries.** Decide content, format, and frequency to report to leadership and incorporate feedback.
- **Templates.** Determine every opportunity to create templates for consistency and efficiency, and focus more on critical thinking.
- **Central Repository.** Create a central location for all change management materials and conversations that all impacted stakeholders can easily access when, where, and how they want.
- **Measurement.** Agree to measurement KPIs, frequency to report results, and approaches for optimization.

As a result of these initial process steps, Lorraine and Bryan gained visibility and credibility with leadership, trust and optimism within each of their team's direct reports, and confidence among themselves to *manage the change process for the transformation process change.*

In the next chapter, we'll return to our Lorraine-Bryan case study and see how they identified stakeholders for their action steps above for their new change management process.

 INSIDER TIP

If you do not have a formal Project Management Office (PMO), that's okay. But you definitely need someone to manage the process, keep the project on schedule, and hold people accountable. Consider bringing in a contract Project Manager to help you get started.

KEY TAKEAWAYS

Let's summarize key takeaways about the change management process for marketing transformations:

1. Include both **human** and **procedural** categories to keep people at the heart of the change and drive transformation adoption effectively and efficiently.
2. Use the power of **templates** to keep the team aligned and focused and the process efficient.
3. **Measure** the impact of your change management to drive transformation sustainability.

I understand the process may feel daunting, especially if this is your first time working with change management. My advice here is to know when to focus your eyes at the top of the staircase (*what you wish to achieve*) versus when to focus on just that one next step in front of you (*what you need to do immediately*, like right now).

Onward to stakeholders. You're doing great. Let's keep going.

*"Bring in the right **people**, at the right time, in the right way."*

—Dina Shapiro

CHAPTER 12

STAKEHOLDERS

Collaborate With the Right People Throughout the Process

"We all need somebody to lean on."
—Bill Withers

 LEARNING OBJECTIVES

After reading this chapter, you will be able to identify relevant stakeholders, determine their roles, and collaborate effectively with your cro

 HOW TO IDENTIFY STAKEHOLDERS

Successful marketing transformation change management plans, processes, and implementation require including **relevant stakeholders**. Marketers need to collaborate with internal and external stakeholders to harness their experience, insight, and perspective.

As I shared in the last chapter, the goal is to **bring in the right people, at the right time, in the right way, for the right reasons.** And I promised that I would share more about this. So here it is...please read this slowly and carefully...

Some people **erroneously** first and only think about which **people** to include on the team. This is when **favoritism** comes into play, or a choice is simply about who you know and like.

If you are one of "the favorite chosen" on the team, well, then everything seems peachy-keen. Or at least, it seems that way *at first*. And it's only good for the group of "favorites." This approach excludes other people, some of whom are more qualified, more interested, and have more value to add.

Bottom line: A high performing team is *not* just based on who you know and like.

We need an objective, fair, thoughtful approach.

Allow me to introduce you to my **Need-Discipline-Person Approach**, which goes like this:

1. Write a list of your **needs.**
2. Match each **need** to a discipline that has the **skills, experience, traits, and perspective.**
3. Assign a **specific person** within each discipline that meets #1 and #2 criteria above.

Let me bring my **Need-Discipline-Person Approach** to life visually to demonstrate.

I listed seven examples below. **Read by the row, left to right.** (Do not read by the column.)

I suggest that you pause after reading each row, count to five, take a couple of deep breaths, and then move on to the next row.

Don't worry, there's nothing bad. It's just a lot to take in.

Check it out on the next page.

THE NEED-DISCIPLINE-PERSON APPROACH: AN EXAMPLE

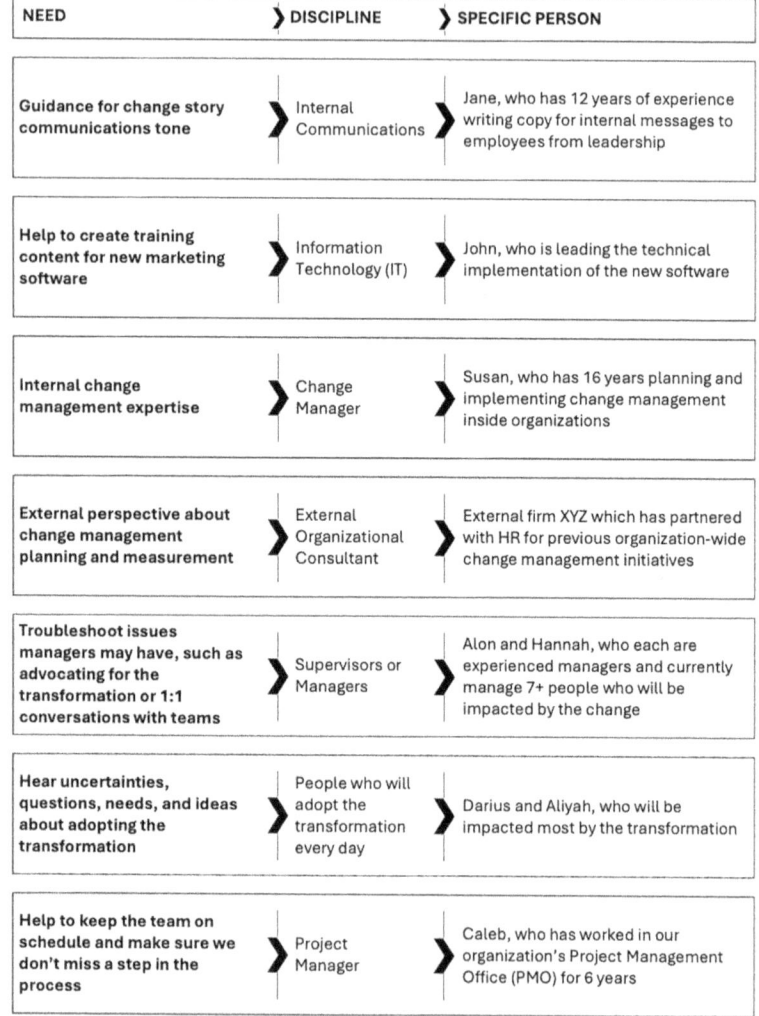

NEED	DISCIPLINE	SPECIFIC PERSON
Guidance for change story communications tone	Internal Communications	Jane, who has 12 years of experience writing copy for internal messages to employees from leadership
Help to create training content for new marketing software	Information Technology (IT)	John, who is leading the technical implementation of the new software
Internal change management expertise	Change Manager	Susan, who has 16 years planning and implementing change management inside organizations
External perspective about change management planning and measurement	External Organizational Consultant	External firm XYZ which has partnered with HR for previous organization-wide change management initiatives
Troubleshoot issues managers may have, such as advocating for the transformation or 1:1 conversations with teams	Supervisors or Managers	Alon and Hannah, who each are experienced managers and currently manage 7+ people who will be impacted by the change
Hear uncertainties, questions, needs, and ideas about adopting the transformation	People who will adopt the transformation every day	Darius and Aliyah, who will be impacted most by the transformation
Help to keep the team on schedule and make sure we don't miss a step in the process	Project Manager	Caleb, who has worked in our organization's Project Management Office (PMO) for 6 years

Here are my Don't and Do lists to help you work through the Need-Discipline-Approach on your own.

DON'T:

- Do not underestimate the importance of identifying the right stakeholders.
- Do not underestimate the time required to create your invitation list.
- Do not assume that everyone will simply say *"Sure! Great! Yes! I'll join your team!"*
- Do not force someone to join your team (that will end badly for sure).
- Do not use the same language or generic approach to invite each person.

DO:

- Make a **personalized, compelling case** for each individual's invitation.
- Share your reason **why** for inviting this person.
- Share the **individual benefits** to each person.
- **Respect** each person's decision, whether they say yes or no to join.

According to the ANA "Marketing Capabilities Framework" study, **"engaging and navigating stakeholders"** is a top desired skill for marketers. So choosing the right team not only improves your likelihood of success for this project, but in my experience and opinion, it also is great for your reputation, performance appraisal, and likelihood to earn a promotion, raise, or bonus. ;)

 # HOW TO DETERMINE ROLES AND RESPONSIBILITIES FOR EACH STAKEHOLDER

Okay, you have the correct range and types of disciplines on your team, and everyone likes and respects one another. That's great, *except* if people are *not* clear about their role on the team. In this case, you've got a pretty big problem, and things can go south very quickly!

Examples of bad things that happen when people are **not clear about their role** include:

Tension	Friction
Frustration	Unclear direction
"We-they" attitude	Work reactively
Poor morale	Lack of active listening and dialogue
Unhealthy debates that shut people down	Less than optimal project outcome
Need to go to multiple places or people to get answers to questions	Nobody "owns" anything, so things don't get done or take much longer
Ambiguity and disagreements about who does what, leading to inaction	Loudest person makes final decisions and others feel like second-class citizens
Short term "get it done" attitude with little thought about medium- and long-term needs or benefits	Blame and finger-pointing when things don't go well (which feels like most of the time)

You can avoid or overcome these problems by creating a **project management framework to assign roles.**

Benefits of a project management framework include:

- Retaining objectivity and fairness
- Leveraging each person's strengths and mitigating each person's weaknesses (we all have both)
- Assessing and evaluating based on established objectives and criteria
- Resolving process ambiguities and different perspectives
- Representing cross-discipline brain power
- Bringing in the right people, for the right item (visibility, opinions, ideas, decisions), at the right time in the process
- Reconciling role conceptions and expectations

Hmm, let's dive into that last point more deeply: **A project management framework reconciles role conceptions, expectations, and behaviors**.

Role **conception** is what a person **thinks** their job is. Someone may have these thoughts because of how they've been taught to do their job, or they may have been influenced by false assumptions, such as a misleading job title or training from a previous supervisor.

Role **expectation** is what **other people in the organization think** someone is responsible for. They may be influenced by incorrect information, such as how it was at a former job, priority changes, or inconsistent leadership direction.

Role **behavior** is what a person actually **does** in their job.

If you pause and think about these three definitions, you may remember times that you've experienced these discrepancies, either for yourself or by one of your colleagues. It's painful when you're knee-deep in this discrepancy. It can feel like you're in quicksand with no way out.

So let me say this again:

> **A project management framework reconciles role conceptions, expectations, and behaviors....**
>
> ...so **behavior** becomes more **predictable** and **productive,** aka, you won't feel like you're sinking in quicksand.

There are lots of project management frameworks out there. If you have a Project Manager on your team, they may suggest an approach. Or check with colleagues to see if your organization uses a specific framework or practice that you're expected to use.

I use RACI because it's a straightforward, understandable, and credible matrix. **RACI** is an acronym for a framework that includes those who are:

- **R**esponsible – The person who **completes the task.** This can be shared by more than one person.

- **A**ccountable – The person who **makes the final decision.** This can be a different person for different steps in the process; however, there can be **only one** person assigned at each step.

- **C**onsulted – The **subject matter expert** who is brought in **prior** to a final decision. It's a **two-way communication.** This can be shared by more than one person and can be shared by different people at different steps in the process.

- Informed – These folks are told **after** actions are taken or decisions are made. It's a **one-way communication**. **No** actions are taken **after** someone is informed.

RACI is best created and shared as a **chart**. For example, your left column lists each step in the process, your top row includes each discipline and person on the team, and then you fill in each empty box with either R, A, C, or I. Place only **one** letter in each box.

I recommend assigning a **facilitator** for **every** meeting. You can rotate, it doesn't need to be the same person for each meeting. Anyone can do it. You don't need any special qualifications or certifications. You do, however, need team agreement about the **facilitator's role**.

Here's how to get started:

1. Think through all **steps** in the process, usually it's in the 10-25 range.

2. Determine which **actions** or **decisions** need to happen for **each** step. Try to avoid sentences that start with generic or nebulous words, like "understand." Use focused, concise, action verbs, like *"complete," "ideate,"* or *"apply feedback."*

3. Assign a **discipline** and **name** for each step. You may have more than one for each step.

4. **Fill in all the empty boxes in your RACI chart.** Typically it helps to start with the "R's," then each "A," and then finish up with "C's" and "I's."

5. Get **team feedback and buy-in.** Start with a team conversation to review the chart with your rationale. Allow people time to think. Provide a deadline to collect or discuss feedback. If someone's idea is not included, tell them why so they do *not* feel ignored and *do* understand your thought process.

An **executive sponsor** should review this completed framework after the team reaches agreement. Your project manager or facilitator should reference this framework when opening and closing each meeting.

Here are some ideas to keep in mind as you complete your project management framework, whether it's RACI or something else. I'll review for both internal disciplines and external partners.

INTERNAL DISCIPLINES

Executive sponsor: An executive sponsor should provide **feedback** and actively **participate** throughout the process. Executive sponsor support increases the probability of a project's success.

Treat your decision about which executive sponsor to approach with great care. There is a substantial difference between an effective and ineffective sponsor. According to Prosci, only 48% have an effective or very effective sponsor on the team! Their research also shows that projects with extremely ineffective sponsors are only 27% likely to meet their objectives as compared to **79% with extremely effective sponsors.** I told you this is a big decision.

You need someone with positive energy, who *advocates* for this transformation, is familiar with and believes in change management best practices, gets the importance of placing *people at the heart of the change*, and is *influential* across levels and disciplines within the organization.

This is what my amazing interviewees shared about executive sponsors:

- *"You need alignment at the leadership level. A consistent vision at the top about where the business needs to go and the role of the executive sponsor can help with this."*

- *"The biggest thing is that you do need a sponsor or visionary or someone who will never give up, who will always ask how's the change, that senior person, the high potentials can report into who really cares that it gets done. Without that, the transformation and the change management will never succeed."*

- *"My company has 800 people. I do think it's important that senior management outside of marketing is supportive and communicates that support. We need that backing for strength and buy-in across the company. That's where an executive sponsor comes in."*

Project Managers: They are experts at existing or required processes in place and how they apply to your project. They can help you create new processes when needed. They ensure accountability to the schedule and by the people.

Learning and Development (L&D) and Trainers: They may be overloaded with organization-wide and mandatory training. Have an open, honest conversation about how, what, and when they can contribute. Ask them about existing resources, such as the Learning Management System (LMS) or vendors. Be clear about requirements versus suggestions. Ask them what breadth and depth of involvement they see for themselves.

HR: They are a great resource for how to incorporate transformation adoption and sustainability in performance objectives and appraisals and how your initiative aligns with broader organizational goals. They are helpful with communications tone and leadership approvals.

Change Managers: Only a few organizations have these wonderful internal practitioners on staff (sigh). If you have them, bring someone in ASAP! You may be able to hire freelance or contract help; check with HR and your supervisor.

Internal Communications: Stay close to this group. They have written and unwritten rules about communicating with employees, such as how, where, or when. It's also good to coordinate timing, such as if they are about to communicate big news organization-wide so messages do not conflict or one message does not overpower the other.

Subject matter experts: Keep this specific to your transformation. For example, if it's a technology transformation, that would be IT.

EXTERNAL PARTNERS

Many organizations use **external** help. According to Gartner, 51% of people undergoing change management use external partners to oversee or participate in aspects of change management.

Let's review a couple of possible *external resources*:

External organizational change management consultants: Their team should have expertise specifically with change management for **marketing transformations.** Include them in your project management framework and all meetings. Confirm if there is an established partner you are required to use, or if you can choose a partner, follow internal rules and processes. Check with your supervisor, HR, procurement, finance, and perhaps legal before you move forward with a partner.

External agency partner: They are a tremendously **under-used resource!** Your agency partner knows your organizational culture and team and has expertise in personas, journey mapping, communications, presentations, training, and selling ideas.

Remember in Chapter 3, when we talked about how **your** marketing skills, experience, and traits are applicable to change management? Well, yeah, you guessed it. Same goes for your agency team. They likely will be affected on some level by your marketing transformation. They are great people to include in marketing transformation change management. (Same goes here for internal agency partners.)

HOW TO COLLABORATE WITH STAKEHOLDERS

Most people agree that **collaboration** benefits the work process. People are more **engaged**, the team benefits from **diverse perspectives and ideas**, each person **learns** more, and the overall **project outcome** is better.

However, we can run into **barriers** to collaboration, such as perceived lack of time, unhealthy organizational culture, no empathy, or the belief that you are collaborating when in fact you are only cooperating. (Any of this sound familiar to you?)

Here's how to **overcome** these barriers and foster **collaboration** with your team:

- Define **roles** and **responsibilities** for clarity throughout the project.
- Get to **know one another,** such as strengths and weaknesses (we all have both), and different personalities and work styles.
- Assign a **facilitator** for each meeting to make sure everyone is heard and respected.
- Stay **close to your executive sponsor** to keep focused on project objectives and assist with leadership buy-in or questions.
- Be **empathetic** to envision the perspectives of other people.
- **Listen actively** to understand what other people are saying (don't just not talk while others are talking while you formulate your response in your head...or get busy on your phone...that's just not cool).
- Be **curious**, ask people how they feel about things, or to tell you more, or to see what they think you can do.
- Differentiate between **cooperation** and **collaboration.**

Okay, let's hit that last point more deeply: **Many people believe they are collaborating when they are only cooperating.** Cooperation isn't necessarily bad, but it is *different* from collaboration. Both cooperation and collaboration are about working with other people.

However, they **differ** in key ways, for example:

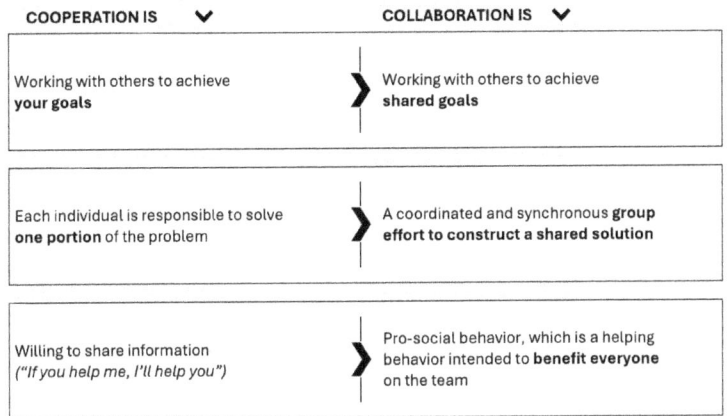

 ## APPLICATION OF WHAT WE HAVE LEARNED:
Collaborating With Your Cross-Discipline Team

Let's return to our Lorraine-Bryan case study from the last chapter. They are creating a *change management process* for a *marketing process* transformation for their bank's credit card LOB. Lorraine is the Senior Project Manager leading change management. Bryan is the CX Director of the CX COE.

Their next step is to identify which **stakeholders** to include in the change management process. Lorraine pulled out her action steps she created regarding the process, which we reviewed in the last chapter.

She and Bryan sat down to determine stakeholders. They started writing down names of those who they thought were smart, hardworking, and would be fun to work with.

LOUD ANNOYING BUZZING SOUND! (Signifying *"WRONG ANSWER!"*)

As Lorraine and Bryan began writing a list of their favorites among who they knew, they realized they were not approaching this correctly!

Enter: Jaime, Head of HR for the bank.

Jaime has excellent relationships with the leadership team and is known to be objective, fair, and empathetic. Jaime has worked in HR for over 20 years at a range of companies.

Lorraine and Bryan scheduled a meeting with Jaime to ask for their help. Together, they decided to use my **Need-Discipline-Person** approach (as described earlier in this chapter). The team first wrote a list of **needs**. Then the team matched each **need** to the appropriate **discipline**. From there, the team reviewed a list of **names** within each discipline.

To choose one name from each discipline, they created a list of **decision criteria** specific to that discipline and what would be needed for the change management team.

Voila! They had their **high-performing** team based on an objective and fair approach, which will facilitate **diversity of thought, creativity, and critical thinking**.

Jaime has a standing invitation to leadership's monthly status meetings. They requested a special addition to the meeting agenda for Lorraine and Bryan to share their recommended team and rationale. The team list was approved.

They took the time to create **personalized invitations** for each person. First, they sent a custom email to each person and then requested a meeting to talk through why they invited that person.

Every person who was invited accepted. Success!

And that's a wrap to our Lorraine-Bryan-Jaime case study.

 INSIDER TIP

You're smack in the middle of your project. Some people on the team think that one person no longer belongs on the team. Before you act (like complaining to their supervisor or kicking them off the team), ask yourself: "*What would we **lose** if this person was no longer on the team?*" Often, we then realize the contributions that this person *has* made or *could* make. It might be a communication challenge, or perhaps a revision to your project management framework may be helpful. Sometimes, a person's role can be **redefined** or **clarified**, and that person will contribute more collaboratively and effectively.

 KEY TAKEAWAYS

Let's summarize key takeaways about collaborating with stakeholders:

1. Use an **objective, thoughtful process** to bring in the **right people**, at the right time, in the right way, for the right reasons.
2. Consider both **internal** and **external** stakeholders.
3. Use **responsibility charting** to ensure clarity of **roles** and facilitate **collaboration** within the cross-discipline team.

Our next and final chapter will guide you through 10 steps for the **first 90 days** of your change management plan. We're in the home stretch!

*"I'm not that special.
I did it, **you** can do it!"*

—Dina Shapiro

CHAPTER 13

10 STEPS FOR YOUR FIRST 90 DAYS:

Ready, Set, Launch!

"The most important decisions you make in your first 90 days will probably be about people."
—Michael D. Watkins

 LEARNING OBJECTIVES

After reading this chapter, you will be able to prepare 10 steps for the first 90 days of your marketing transformation change management plan.

 10 STEPS FOR YOUR FIRST 90 DAYS

Welcome to our final chapter! You've just read a ton of information. I want you to feel comfortable getting started.

1. **People first.** Remember the people who will implement the changes every day. Place *people* at the *heart* of the transformation. Believe me when I tell you that your change management plan is *nothing without the people*. Listen. Respect. Respond. Maintain an open dialogue. Be transparent. Bring people in *early* and *nurture* the relationship to sustain the transformation.

2. **Trust your brainpower and intuition.** Review the notes you wrote in each chapter about what you learned and what you will *do new or differently*. If you didn't take notes while you were reading, that's okay! Go back now and do a quick once-over of each chapter and write down your thoughts and ideas. Check out the worksheets I provided at the end of this chapter.

3. **Create your process.** Review previous chapters. Pull together your *cross-discipline team* of internal and external stakeholders and subject matter experts. Write key action steps and a schedule. Apply project management best practices. Assign and get buy-in for each team member's roles and responsibilities.

4. **Create your change management plan.** Align change management objectives with higher level objectives of the transformation and organizational goals. Do internal research to discover relevant employee insights. Create employee personas and Change Journey Maps including stages, messaging, and touch points. Write an insightful, actionable Change Management Brief. Create your inspiring and engaging change story and experience. Measure and optimize.

5. **Test before you launch.** Pull together a small representative sample of people who will need to implement the changes. Run an abbreviated test with select change story communications and experiences such as training or resources. Obtain feedback, revise as needed, and then launch. Your launch still won't be perfect because life isn't perfect. You likely will need to optimize along the way, but your launch will go *much more smoothly!*

6. **Apply best practices from sports.** You don't need to be a superstar athlete or sports fan to do this. Keep your eye on the ball. Follow through. Maintain your focus; don't get distracted. Don't get cocky. Don't let a little "booing" from the audience get you down. "Booing" will happen no matter how hard you work and no matter how great your work is. Find out the reason for the "booing" and address it openly and honestly to the best of your ability. When you miss a shot, *pick yourself up*, and *concentrate on the next shot.*

7. **Empathy is sacred.** It's totally cool to have your own perspective and ideas. Just don't operate in a vacuum. Empathy is the ability to envision other people's perspectives. Remember the two E's: **E**mpathy = to **E**nvision the other person's perspective.

8. **Learn objection handling.** In our context, this is about addressing people's concerns throughout their change journey so you can help them get from one stage to the next, through adoption to sustainability of the marketing transformation. There's a ton of research you can read online about objection handling, which

primarily is geared toward salespeople. But you, my brilliant marketers, are more than capable to make the leap and *apply* from that research what's *relevant* to change management for marketing transformations.

9. **Get to "The Click."** I wish I could take credit for this one, but I can't. As one of my interviewees said so well, **"The Click is that point where you really land the plane. People are incredulous along the journey until it clicks. The Click is the magic point where people can suspend the past and get on the bus. But that takes practice and poking. You won't get it 100% right out the door."** (How perfect is that?)

10. **Find your confidence and courage.** They are inside you; I promise. Remember that marketers are *uniquely qualified* to lead change management for marketing transformations. **Nobody can do this better than you.**

 ## BRINGING IT TO LIFE

Okay, so here is my **final list of quotes from my amazing interviewees**. Ideas to drive **success** during the **first 90 days** of change management for a marketing transformation include:

- *"Get the story right. Need someone who will thread all the elements together in the plan so it sounds like a reasonable story. This does not happen in the beginning. Practice articulating different things to different people in different ways. It will happen by moving the elements around an actual story that you want. It's about speaking in the attitude, having the courage to express yourself in a way that it will resonate with those who you are trying to bring along."*

- *"Talk in a real way. Talk it through with the team. Let people feel your energy and real-ness."*

- *"The first 90 days are critical. Or more like the first 30 days. Need buy-in, traction, otherwise it will die on a vine."*

- *"Use weekly check-ins for people to rally around. Don't be afraid to assign homework, like pre-reading, or things for people to think about in advance of a meeting."*

- *"There are people who won't make the change and you know it just won't work. Don't feel badly and keep people around too long. You need to take care of this quickly. Don't wait."*

- *"Choose external partners wisely."*

- *"Set expectations, it's never smooth; this isn't plug in and play. This won't cure everything, but let people know what this transformation can accomplish."*

- *"Use monthly marketing calls. Include updates on the changes and impacts to the team. Share results from measurement of the new ways of doing things. How are things coming along. What's the ROI?"*

- *"Really get everyone to understand what problem we are trying to solve and get agreement. Then outline how this tool can solve this problem or chip away at the problem over time. Make sure people understand the why. You need to get that message out there. Like, we are doing this because we have a problem that impacts our business, so we need to address it."*

- *"People want to know, what about me? So the change story needs to be tailored, especially through different levels of tool development. Town Hall, kick it off, have another meeting throughout the process, and always end with 'here's what we ask of you.' Then, after 90 days, share what we've learned and how we may change how we are teaching you. So you know, people feel that their feedback is being heard."*

- *"Measure where you are now. Describe where you want to be and what are those metrics to track to where we want to be. Then break down the journey into gate-posted smart steps. Each step becomes a sprint."*

- *"Educate everybody involved in what's coming. Take the time to make sure that everyone understands what is coming down to their daily changes. Also, spend more time just talking to people, understand where they are in their openness to change. And craft a clear communication strategy around the change management including how we will measure success. Bring people along. Tell them what the training program is and how long this will continue. Too many times the end of the project is the end of the change management initiative, but people are still going through their change curve after implementation."*

- *"Help people understand what's changing and why. What's the scale and impact of this change? What's the timing? What does it mean for what you do, how you work? What are the implications or impact to employees, customers, investors, shareholders, regulators, the full 360 of impact? What are the three most important messages to convey about that change? Then build out a framework that will lead to more questions to get to the next level."*

- *"Get alignment on overall objectives and goals and how this transformation will help drive broader business dimensions, or if it's just cost savings, or deepen relationships, whatever—get that alignment. You need that point that you keep going back to—it's in pursuit of this goal—continuously ask, 'Is what we are doing in pursuit of that goal?' Commitment needs to extend beyond the marketing organization itself because marketing touches others so you need to partner and work with others. This does not just sit within the marketing organization."*

- *"Enrollment, which involves vision and the why behind the change and acknowledgement of the anticipated negative ramifications of it. A clear set of steps that will be taken so it's not all at once, which needs to make sense to people, like, why this first, or this next. Feedback mechanism is built into the system because there will be some aspects that were not right and need to adjust, and it provides a credible basis where everyone feels that their input is valued. So if they have a meaningful obstacle, there is a formal feedback loop for unanticipated meaningful problems which are expected to surface even if we don't know what they are. You need a mechanism in place to address this unforeseen hiccup."*

- *"I love the idea of involving people early on. Have a Town Hall, and share, this is the problem we are trying to solve, these are the things we are thinking, let us know if this is what you all think, or if we are missing anything before we embark on the change. Don't only ask management or leadership. Ask the people in the everyday weeds for the accurate read."*

- *"Sometimes, people romance this thing called change management as this flip-the-switch ideal. But maybe it is a little more gradual, more butterfly-ish, like from a caterpillar to the butterfly."*

And there you have it, my friends.

 **INSIDER TIP**

Here are some **reminders** to help you **stay on course** throughout your change management initiative, especially those moments when you *may feel down or doubtful*:

- Listen to others.
- Embrace change.
- Be open and curious.
- Adapt strategies or tactics quickly.
- Be an active, empathetic listener.
- Adopt a lifelong learner approach every day.
- Get comfortable taking risks. As Wayne Gretzky said, *"You miss 100% of the shots you don't take."*

 KEY TAKEAWAYS

Let's summarize key takeaways about 10 steps for the first 90 days of your marketing transformation change management plan:

1. **You got this!**
2. Stay close to the **people**; you simply cannot do this on your own.
3. I want you to remember, always, **that marketers are uniquely qualified to lead change management for marketing transformations...Nobody can do this better than you!**

I have provided three worksheets on the next three pages:

1. Taking Action: What Did You Learn?
2. Taking Action: What Will You Do Differently?
3. Your 10-Step Plan

TAKING ACTION:
What did you learn?

WHAT DID YOU LEARN IN THIS BOOK THAT YOU CAN IMPLEMENT IN YOUR OWN WORKPLACE?

TAKING ACTION:
What Will You Do Differently?

WHAT WILL YOU DO NEW OR DIFFERENTLY IN YOUR WORKPLACE?

FROM ⟶ TO

>

🔟 YOUR 10 STEP PLAN

STEP	ACTION	TIMING
1		
2		
3		
4		
5		
6		
7		
8		
9		
10		

THOUGHTS ABOUT AI
(Artificial Intelligence)

Fact: No AI was used to write this book.

Here's why:

1. I knew people would ask me this question. I wanted to be able to answer "*No*."
2. Even if I wanted to use AI, it would *not have been possible*. AI collects and summarizes information *currently* available on the internet. When I wrote this book, there were *no* books, articles, studies, etc. on this subject even remotely close to my approach.

As you read this book, you may have seen opportunities to use AI-powered tools, such as to summarize research insights, visualize personas, personalize communications, or choose touch points. That's cool.

I encourage you to use AI-powered tools to **automate collecting and summarizing information**. It's **faster** and **easier** than manual research, so you have *more time* to think about *insights*, *implications*, and *recommended actions*.

Here are a few thoughts to keep in mind if you use AI-powered tools to create your change management plan for marketing transformations:

- **AI is like your best friend who thinks they know everything. —Elvin Flores.** If you ask AI a question, you will receive a response. It just may not be *the best response.*

- **The output is only as good as the input.** *How* you phrase a question matters immensely. If two people use the same AI tool and alter the same question by one word, the two AI responses will likely be different. Use your *human brain* to ask questions that maximize AI's responses and accuracy.

- **Use AI as a springboard.** It can help you get started and provide initial ideas; however, it is *not* the end-all-be-all.

- **Your human brain is best, so keep yourself involved in the process.** Apply critical thinking to AI summaries to *evaluate, question,* and *solve problems.* Remember, AI frees up your time from boring manual tasks so you can spend *more* time on the juicy, interesting stuff.

- **Stay on top of AI tools, capabilities, and vendors.** I feel like this information changes by the second, but we all need to stay current on what's available, benefits, and cautions such as privacy, bias, and transparency.

That's all I have to say about AI, at least in this book.

LET'S STAY IN TOUCH

Congratulations!

Thank you for reading *Change Management for Marketers: Internal Transformations Made Easy*.

Contact me, Dina Shapiro, for speaking, training, and consulting at: hello@yorkvilleconsulting.com.

Follow me on LinkedIn at: https://www.linkedin.com/in/shapirodina/.

If you found this book helpful, please share testimonials and pictures of you with this book in social media and review this book wherever you purchased it.

ACKNOWLEDGEMENTS

To you, the **reader**, thank *you*. This book, all the hours, all the late writing nights, and all the conversations that went into it, were worth it because you chose to read it.

A heartfelt thank you to all my **interviewees** who took time out of their crazy busy days to thoughtfully and honestly answer every single one of my questions. All my interviewees hold bigwig executive and senior positions at large and publicly held companies, so they could only participate anonymously. You all know who you are. Thank you. I simply could not have written this book without your brilliant insights.

Thank you, **Michelle**. You were the first person to read my manuscript other than my publisher and editor. I asked you to read just the two-page Introduction. About 15 minutes later (a long time to read only two pages), you were still reading. I was terrified! I said, *"Oh no, you hate it."* You looked up from the computer, and said, *"No, I'm already on Chapter 4."* You stayed at my desk and read the entire draft. Your compliments and encouragement psyched me up to keep going, and meant more to me than I can ever explain to you.

Thank you, **Nancy**. You were excited for me from the first moment that I shared the subject of this book. You helped me with your marketing transformation technology and data insights and expertise.

Thank you, **Denise**. I asked you to read just a few pages from my iPhone over lunch. You not only liked what you read, but you explained in detail *why* you thought this would be a great book. You definitely would have told me if you thought it was awful. I was relieved and excited to hear your supportive words. That lunch kept me going.

Thank you, **Nicole Mené**. My dear friend who left this world and all your loved ones way too soon. You taught me not to take changes in my professional life personally, to just focus on what needs to get done, and move forward. I did my best to share that valuable lesson in this book.

Thank you to everyone who read my manuscript and shared your compliments that have been quoted as advanced praise blurbs on the inside cover of the book.

Thank you, all my previous and current **colleagues, clients,** and **students.** My experience with you helped shape me professionally and my ability to write this book.

Thank you, **Andrew Robertson**, Chairman BBDO Worldwide. On July 20th, 2012 (yes, 2012), in your office at 1285 Avenue of the Americas, you suggested, "*Write a book, get published.*" Okay, it took me a while to figure out something worthwhile to write about, but I did it.

Thank you to my publisher, **Thin Leaf Press**, and editor, **Erik Seversen**, who helped me navigate this process. I could not have written, finished, and published this book without your encouragement, patience, and positive energy.

Thank you, **Hugh**, my love and hottie-hot-hots, who put up with all the times I woke up in the middle of the night to write down ideas that came to me during my sleep. Whenever I ran an idea by you, you listened.

Mom, thank you for believing that I could do this and never doubting my abilities. **Dad**, I know you are looking down from above, proud of me.

I'm profoundly grateful to **all my family and friends** who believed in me, and encouraged and supported me every step of the way, whether you knew it or not! I am eternally grateful. I love you.

If I missed you on this list, tell me. I'll take you to lunch and thank you personally.

SOURCES CONSULTED

MARKETING TRANSFORMATIONS

Definition and Examples

- Cambridge Dictionary, definition of transformation, https://dictionary.cambridge.org/us/dictionary/english/transformation
- Merriam-Webster Dictionary, definition of transformation, https://www.merriam-webster.com/dictionary/transformation

Chapter 1

CHANGE MANAGEMENT

What Is It and Why Does It Matter?

- Google search, "Definition of Change Management"
- Gartner, "Change Management Strategy for Marketers," 2023, https://www.gartner.com/en/human-resources/insights/organizational-change-management#:~:text=Yet%20half%20of%20change%20initiatives,34%25%20are%20a%20clear%20success

- Harvard Business Review, "The Secret Behind Successful Corporate Transformations," September 14, 2021, https://hbr.org/2021/09/the-secret-behind-successful-corporate-transformations
- McKinsey & Company, "Why Do Most Transformations Fail? A Conversation with Harry Robinson," July 10, 2019, https://www.mckinsey.com/capabilities/transformation/our-insights/why-do-most-transformations-fail-a-conversation-with-harry-robinson

Chapter 2
THE HUMAN CHEMISTRY OF CHANGE
How to Overcome Fear of Marketing Transformations

- Cambridge Dictionary, definition of chemistry, https://dictionary.cambridge.org/us/dictionary/english/chemistry
- Merriam-Webster Dictionary, definition of chemistry, https://www.merriam-webster.com/dictionary/chemistry
- NPR "Science Diction: The Origin of 'Chemistry'," August 26, 2011, https://www.npr.org/transcripts/139972673
- School of Public Health, University of Michigan, Faculty Profile, Howard Markel PhD, MD, https://sph.umich.edu/faculty-profiles/markel-howard.html
- NIH (National Institutes of Health) National Library of Medicine, https://www.nlm.nih.gov/about/index.html
- NIH (National Institutes of Health) National Library of Medicine, "The Uncertainty of Errors: Intolerance of Uncertainty is Associated with Error-Related Brain Activity," January 2016, https://pubmed.ncbi.nlm.nih.gov/26607441/

Chapter 3
MARKETERS ARE UNIQUELY QUALIFIED TO LEAD
How to Apply Your Marketing Talents

- Merriam-Webster Dictionary, definition of skill, https://www.merriam-webster.com/dictionary/skill
- Merriam-Webster Dictionary, definition of experience, https://www.merriam-webster.com/dictionary/experience
- Merriam-Webster Dictionary, definition of trait, https://www.merriam-webster.com/dictionary/trait
- Helen Riess, M.D., Founder, Chief Medical Officer, Empathetics, Inc. Harvard Psychiatrist, https://www.linkedin.com/in/helen-riess/
- The Association of National Advertisers (ANA), "The 2023 Marketing Capabilities Framework"

Chapter 4
WHAT HAPPENS WHEN MARKETERS LEAD
Everyone Benefits!

- Gartner, "Change Management Strategy for Marketers," 2023, https://www.gartner.com/en/human-resources/insights/organizational-change-management#:~:text=Yet%20half%20of%20change%20initiatives,34%25%20are%20a%20clear%20success
- Heidrick & Struggles, https://www.heidrick.com/en/about-us
- "Business Talent Group 2024 High-End Independent Talent Report, Securing the Optimal Mix of Skills, Capacity, and Expertise," https://resources.businesstalentgroup.com/high-end-independent-talent-report/talent-trends-2024?utm_medium=Email&utm_

source=Talent%20eBlast&utm_campaign=2024%20
High-End%20Independent%20Talent%20Report&utm_
content=Text&mkt_tok=NTc5LUtLVC00OTgAAAGSYlimItz
9lflzSlNfqSQ5zl7UBsplrWl3Ym2pqfNQSyjamyj8U36NjFw
D8sQ9co0Wd92anvZrkm-13yQqKTis7nuYCQ9rNv3cigTpX
WQuHeBf8g

Chapter 5
EMPLOYEE PERSONAS
How to Personalize Change Communications

- Gallup, https://www.gallup.com/corporate/212381/who-we-are.aspx
- Gallup, "What Is Employee Engagement and How Do You Improve It," https://www.gallup.com/workplace/285674/improve-employee-engagement-workplace.aspx
- Cambridge Dictionary, definition of motivations, https://dictionary.cambridge.org/dictionary/english/motivation?q=motivations
- Cambridge Dictionary, definition of expectations, https://dictionary.cambridge.org/dictionary/english/expectation?q=expectations
- Cambridge Dictionary, definition of attitudes, https://dictionary.cambridge.org/dictionary/english/attitude?q=attitudes
- Cambridge Dictionary, definition of behaviors, https://dictionary.cambridge.org/dictionary/english/behavior?q=behaviors
- Merriam-Webster Dictionary, definition of motivations, https://www.merriam-webster.com/dictionary/motivations

- Merriam-Webster Dictionary, definition of expectations, https://www.merriam-webster.com/dictionary/expectations
- Merriam-Webster Dictionary, definition of attitudes, https://www.merriam-webster.com/dictionary/attitudes
- Merriam-Webster Dictionary, definition of behaviors, https://www.merriam-webster.com/dictionary/behaviors
- Business Journal, "Companywide Communication: Key to Strengths Development" 2016, https://news.gallup.com/businessjournal/196589/companywide-communication-key-strengths-development.aspx
- Calm blog, "How to Build Emotional Connection in Relationships," https://www.calm.com/blog/emotional-connection#:~:text=A%20deep%20emotional%20connection%20with,a%20deep%20bond%20with%20others

Chapter 6
THE EMPLOYEE CHANGE JOURNEY
Map Out the Ride and the Destination

- Cambridge Dictionary, definition of framework, https://dictionary.cambridge.org/dictionary/english/framework
- Merriam-Webster Dictionary, definition of framework, https://www.merriam-webster.com/dictionary/framework

Chapter 7
CHANGE JOURNEY STAGES
Engage Employees Early and Keep That Relationship Going

- Cambridge Dictionary, definition of stage, https://dictionary.cambridge.org/dictionary/english/stage

- Cambridge Dictionary, definition of phase, https://dictionary.cambridge.org/dictionary/english/phase
- Cambridge Dictionary, definition of experience, https://dictionary.cambridge.org/dictionary/english/experience
- Cambridge Dictionary, definition of sequence, https://dictionary.cambridge.org/dictionary/english/sequence
- Merriam-Webster Dictionary, definition of stage, https://www.merriam-webster.com/dictionary/stage
- Merriam-Webster Dictionary, definition of phase, https://www.merriam-webster.com/dictionary/phase
- Merriam-Webster Dictionary, definition of experience, https://www.merriam-webster.com/dictionary/experience
- Merriam-Webster Dictionary, definition of sequence, https://www.merriam-webster.com/dictionary/sequence
- Kurt Lewin's Three Stage Change Process, https://en.wikipedia.org/wiki/Kurt_Lewin
- Kotter's Eight Stage Change Process, https://www.kotterinc.com/methodology/8-steps/
- Prosci ADKAR https://www.prosci.com/
- The Burke–Litwin Change Model, University of Exeter, https://www.exeter.ac.uk/media/universityofexeter/humanresources/documents/learningdevelopment/understanding_drivers_for_change.pdf
- PDCA cycle, https://blog.hubspot.com/marketing/pdca-cycle-model and https://en.wikipedia.org/wiki/PDCA#:~:text=The%20cycle%20is%20sometimes%20referred,Telephone%20Laboratories%20in%20the%201920s
- LinkedIn "What are the Pros and Cons of Using a Linear vs. a Circular Change Model?" https://www.linkedin.com/advice/0/what-pros-cons-using-linear-vs-circular-change

Chapter 8
CHANGE JOURNEY MESSAGING
Speak To the Heart and the Head

- Cambridge Dictionary, definition of communicate, https://dictionary.cambridge.org/dictionary/english/communicate
- Merriam-Webster Dictionary, definition of communicate, https://www.merriam-webster.com/dictionary/communicate
- Cleveland Clinic HealthEssentials, "Left Brain vs. Right Brain: Are You Really One or the Other?," May 2023, https://health.clevelandclinic.org/left-brain-vs-right-brain

Chapter 9
CHANGE JOURNEY TOUCH POINTS
Communicate with Employees Where They Want

- Cambridge Dictionary, definition of interact, https://dictionary.cambridge.org/dictionary/english/interact
- Oxford English Dictionary, definition of interact, https://www.oed.com/search/dictionary/?scope=Entries&q=interact

Chapter 10
THE CHANGE MANAGEMENT BRIEF
Create an Honest, Open, and Real Change Story

- "Inversion and the Power of Avoiding Stupidity," https://fs.blog/inversion/
- "Charlie Munger: Wit and Wisdom from the World's Most Irreverent Billionaire," https://fs.blog/intellectual-giants/charlie-munger/

- "Charlie Munger on the Value of Thinking Backward and Forward," https://fs.blog/charlie-munger-thinking-backward-forward/
- About FS, https://fs.blog/about/
- The New York Times, "How a Former Canadian Spy Helps Wall Street Mavens Think Smarter," 11/11/2018, https://www.nytimes.com/2018/11/11/business/intelligence-expert-wall-street.html

Chapter 11
THE CHANGE MANAGEMENT PROCESS
Place People at the Heart of the Marketing Transformation

- National Geographic, "Changes in Matter: Physical vs. Chemical Changes," https://education.nationalgeographic.org/resource/changes-matter-physical-vs-chemical-changes/
- HR Today, "New Research: 43% of Employees Don't feel Valued by their Employer," 10/10/23, https://www.hrotoday.com/news/new-research-43-of-employees-dont-feel-valued-by-their-employer/#:~:text=Employer%20%2D%20HRO%20Today-,New%20Research%3A%2043%25%20of%20Employees%20Don't%20Feel%20Valued,lack%20of%20action%20from%20employers
- Deloitte, "Workforce listening: The Proof Is in the Planning," April 20, 2023, https://action.deloitte.com/insight/3303/workforce-listening-the-proof-is-in-the-planning
- BCG, "Is Your Upskilling Program Paying Off?," January 30, 2024, https://www.bcg.com/publications/2024/is-your-upskilling-program-paying-off?utm_

campaign=none&utm_content=202402&utm_
description=featured_insights&utm_geo=global&utm_
medium=email&utm_source=esp&utm_topic=futureof
work&utm_usertoken=4e551fdde9f6e8d8ff7820f8241bb
47232549c5 b&mkt_tok=Nzk5LUlPQi04ODMAAAGRTBm0
Kbp-fZWTI71Qs21z PwEwlz9uoakUzKWepHhOy0mS6rgA
QblOxS54SoTqNQd25m57YFwXnDvQTw0_5V9QKavGkRO
qQc-9vefLjMW0HXs

- Prosci, "Metrics for Measuring Change Management,"
March 26, 2024, https://www.prosci.com/blog/
metrics-for-measuring-change-management?utm_
campaign=%5BEN-ALL%5D%20Blog%20Email%20
Outreach%202024&utm_medium=email&_
hsmi=300156970&_hsenc=p2ANqtz--j-f7PnR-
74deoW6kOhUwVzFsIEl_Y5FQcHtCT7oTc-XVk4suCA8OH
7BBEGNartSNKHkoBeMY5e4ndvU7kqyEvpTUZqglTuDU_
Kb4HaYR7hmgKhf0&utm_content=299986830&utm_
source=hs_email
- Prosci, "The Strategic Imperative of Sustainment
in Change Management," March 12, 2024,
https://www.prosci.com/blog/sustainment-in-
change-management?utm_campaign=%5BEN-
ALL%5D%20Blog%20Email%20Outreach%20
2024&utm_medium=email&_hsmi=298117971&_
hsenc=p2ANqtz--GzHUGP3L4OON1l-
gmK5TSrHhCF-YFbS-VGycZ354ItjNm6TB1WmwaXY-
Nu9j9wXf20eLFISzwxiJqXQp2CyjtKwn16-
Kw1QM95x2dWsxmGESOgcQ&utm_
content=297925954&utm_source=hs_email

Chapter 12
STAKEHOLDERS
Collaborate With the Right People Throughout the Process

- The Association of National Advertisers (ANA), "The 2023 Marketing Capabilities Framework"
- Prosci, "Best Practices in Change Management," 7/19/24, https://www.prosci.com/blog/change-management-best-practices?utm_campaign=%5BEN-US%5D%20Novice%20CP%20%7C%20Certification%20 Nurture%20program%20%7C%20Ongoing&utm_medium=email&_hsmi=98117758&_hsenc=p2ANqtz--zVDQASHFjHnN5-G3QGMX1ZWBhwhvzKEHCL BzvssqPcBOY525CBC4Ha7zxnI7f5mEWWDINM1 ULMa2-xTFgblsInfosjX2bz1JSHIrTrsUd_5wEQnY& utm_content=98117758&utm_source=hs_automation
- Gartner, "Change Management Strategy for Marketers," 2023, https://www.gartner.com/en/ human-resources/insights/organizational-change-management#:~:text=Yet%20half%20of%20change%20 initiatives,34%25%20are%20a%20clear%20success

Chapter 13
A 10 POINT PLAN FOR YOUR FIRST 90 DAYS
Ready, Set, Launch!

- "From-To" Worksheet, Sullivan, Nicole Ferry

ALL CHAPTERS
Icons designed by Freepik; www.freepik.com

ABOUT
THE AUTHOR

Dina Shapiro is a Change Management and Marketing speaker, trainer, and consultant.

She is the Founder of Yorkville Consulting, a WBENC certified woman-owned business since 2013 that has won over 35 industry awards. She has worked with over 200 clients, mostly Fortune 500 companies, to help them with change management and marketing consulting and training.

Previously, Dina was the Senior Vice President and Director for Fortune 125 companies Citi and Alcoa, where she led marketing communications, brand strategy, change management, and training. Before that, she was an ad agency executive at BBDO and J. Walter Thompson (now VML), where she led strategy and campaign development for iconic brands that won multiple industry awards.

She has multiple published LinkedIn Learning courses with several language translations that have been viewed, liked, and shared by hundreds of thousands of people globally.

Dina teaches three courses in New York University's MS in Integrated Marketing program as a top-rated Adjunct Assistant Professor.

She holds an MBA in General Management from Boston University Questrom School of Business and a BA in Economics from George Washington University.

Dina lives in her beloved New York City with her loving and supportive partner Hugh, who reminds her every day to find the humor in life, and Izzy, the cutest, sweetest, funniest, most snuggly dog imaginable.

Did You Enjoy This Book?

If you enjoyed reading this book, you can help by suggesting it to someone else you think might like it, and **please leave a positive review** wherever you purchased it. This does a lot in helping others find the book. We thank you in advance for taking a few moments to do this.

Thank you.

Other Thin Leaf Press Titles

Peak Performance: Mindset Tools for Managers

Peak Performance: Mindset Tools for Sales

Peak Performance: Mindset Tools for Leaders

Peak Performance: Mindset Tools for Business

Peak Performance: Mindset Tools for Entrepreneurs

The Successful Mind

Winning Mindset: Elite Strategies for Peak Performance

Winner's Mindset: Peak Performance Strategies for Success

Behind the Queen's Smile

What If Pigs Can Fly?

The AI Mindset

www.ingramcontent.com/pod-product-compliance
Lightning Source LLC
Chambersburg PA
CBHW061738120626
46550CB00005B/1824